Institutionally Funded Student Financial Aid

Institutionally Funded Student Financial Aid

Nathan Dickmeyer
John Wessels
Sharon L. Coldren

AMERICAN COUNCIL ON EDUCATION
Washington, D. C.

© 1981 by American Council on Education
One Dupont Circle, Washington, D.C. 20036

Library of Congress Cataloging in Publication Data

Dickmeyer, Nathan.
    Institutionally funded student financial aid.

    Includes bibliographical references.
    1. Student aid—United States.   I. Wessels, John.
II. Coldren, Sharon L.   III. American Council on
Education.   IV. Title.
LB2337.4.D5   378'.3'0973   81-12819
ISBN 0-8268-1459-X   AACR2

9 8 7 6 5 4 3 2 1
Printed in the United States of America

Contents

Figures and Tables vii

Preface ix

Introduction xi

I. Institutionally Funded Student Aid and Institutional Policy Issues 1

II. Institutionally Funded Student Aid and Equal Educational Opportunity 16

III. Institutionally Funded Student Aid and Selective Recruitment of Students 30

IV. Institutionally Funded Student Aid and Institutional Vitality 40

V. Institutionally Funded Student Work Programs and Tuition Remissions 55

VI. Institutionally Funded Student Aid and Federal Policy Issues 65

Appendix: Federal Student Aid Programs 77

Figures and Tables

Figures

1.1 Iterative pricing model   5

4.1 Hypothetical relationship between perceived cost of a private liberal arts level II institution and the probability of attending the institution   41

4.2 Hypothetical relationship between revenue, enrollment, and net price of a private liberal arts level II institution   43

4.3 Student market study—plot of mean family income versus standard deviation of student family income for three possible situations   44

Tables

A Percent distribution of forms of undergraduate student aid, 1976–77, by sources of aid   xiii

1.1 Percent distribution of institutional grants and loans to freshmen, distributed according to high school grades   10

2.1 Percent and dollar distribution of forms of institutionally funded undergraduate aid, 1976–77, by institutional control   19

2.2 Percent distribution of institutionally funded need-based, merit, and athletic grants, 1976–77, by institutional type and control   20

2.3 Percent distribution of institutionally funded undergraduate grants, 1978–79, by institutional type and control and by tuition level   21

2.4 Average amount of undergraduate institutionally funded student aid, tuition, fees, room and board, 1976–77, by category of institution   22

2.5 Number of institutional grants and tuition remissions, as a percentage of grants awarded to freshmen, 1978–79, by year in school   23

viii *Figures and Tables*

2.6 Enrollment in higher education for each class, as percentage of freshmen, 1978–79, by year in school   24
2.7 Percent distribution of dependent undergraduate student aid recipients, by unadjusted gross family income and source of aid, 1976–77   24
2.8 Percent distribution of dependent undergraduate student aid recipients, by unadjusted gross family income, source of aid, and control, 1976–77   25
2.9 Percent distribution of student aid awards to first-time, full-time freshmen, by level of family income, 1976–77   27
2.10 Distribution of student aid awards, by family income   28

3.1 Percent distribution of the forms of institutionally funded undergraduate student aid, by source of aid, 1976–77   30
3.2 Peaks and troughs in size of particular age groups, 1978–2000   32
3.3 Percent and dollar distribution of forms of institutionally funded undergraduate student aid, 1976–77, by institutional control   33
3.4 Institutions that provided financial inducements for accepted applicants to enroll   34
3.5 Distribution of institutionally funded undergraduate grants and tuition remissions, 1978–79, by institutional type and control   35
3.6 Reasons cited by students for receiving aid, as percentage of students receiving institutional aid   37
3.7 Percent distribution of type of institutionally funded aid to freshmen, by high school grade averages, 1976–77   37

4.1 Reasons given by freshmen for attending a particular institution, by level of importance   48
4.2 Number of four-year independent colleges (non-university) making changes in amount of aid from unrestricted funds, FY 1975 to FY 1978   50
4.3 Average amount of institutionally funded undergraduate student aid, by category of institution, 1976–77   53

5.1 Distribution of institutionally funded student aid: employment programs and tuition remissions   55

Preface

This study is primarily directed to student financial aid policy makers in various levels of government and in individual institutions of higher education who devise and evaluate financial aid programs for college and university students. The purpose of the work is to show how institutions make use of financial aid derived from institutional funds, especially aid from unrestricted general funds.

Student aid programs are funded by both levels of government—federal and state—and by the institutions themselves, and these programs do interact to some degree. As a result, federal and state regulations concerning the award of aid can change an institution's incentives for awarding its own funds. This monograph attempts to inform both institutional and governmental policy makers about the scope and role of institutionally funded student aid. Further, it underscores the need for institutions to continue to allocate institutional funds for financial assistance to their students.

This work is also intended for institutional policy makers who wish to know the national dimensions of institutionally funded student aid programs. The first chapter includes a discussion of important policy options that institutional administrators must consider when awarding institutionally funded student aid.

This project has been supported in large part by the Exxon Education Foundation. In addition, the Lilly Foundation has provided supplemental support.

Introduction

American colleges and universities have always been an important source of financial assistance to students; indeed, for many years they were the only source of such aid. Colleges and universities provide grants to needy students, reward students for academic achievements and other types of achievements, and provide emergency assistance to students in financial difficulty.

In recent years, aid from colleges and universities—referred to here as institutionally funded student financial aid—has received less public attention because both federal and state governments have provided increasing amounts of financial aid to help eliminate the economic barriers for any person wishing to attend a college or university. This development might seem to diminish the need for institutionally funded financial aid, but the rising costs of providing postsecondary education and, hence, the rising tuition costs have in fact heightened the importance of institutionally funded student financial assistance. Funds provided through public aid programs, although substantial, are still insufficient to cover the requests for student financial aid. Institutionally funded student aid augments the funds from these programs and makes up 30 percent of all aid. For every two students who receive aid from federal or state funds, three receive aid from institutional funds. Institutionally funded student aid is, in fact, the precedent for the development of all publicly funded student aid.

The majority of students attending colleges and universities supplement their family's resources with funds from other sources. Tuition, room and board, and other costs are paid through a complex combination of funds from an array of donors and lenders. Some

xii *Introduction*

types of financial aid—veterans' educational benefits, for example—go directly to the student, leaving him or her responsible for allocating these funds for tuition and living expenses. Other types of student financial aid allotted to institutions from government or private sources carry restrictions concerning the eligibility of students and the use of the funds. A third type of aid comes directly from the institution's unrestricted revenues. Thus, financial aid to supplement a family's contribution may be awarded to the student in three ways: (1) it may be awarded directly to the student; (2) it may be awarded to the student through the institution's funds restricted for financial aid; or (3) it may be awarded to the student through the institution's unrestricted funds.[1] Many students receive two or more of these types of aid.

Institutionally funded student aid may be drawn from two categories of institutional funds: restricted funds and unrestricted funds. Both kinds of funds come from three primary sources: (1) the institution's own unrestricted, general funds; (2) endowment income restricted to student financial aid; and (3) private gifts restricted to student financial aid.

Institutionally funded student aid does not include aid funded by government agencies or aid that does not pass through the institution. In general, institutionally funded student aid is awarded on the basis of criteria established independently by the individual institution.

Institutionally funded student aid may be used for tuition, room and board, and other expenses, or it may be limited to tuition. The aid may be allocated in the form of grants, loans, or wages for work performed for the institution.

Many types of aid are currently available to persons who wish to attend a college or university. Federal aid is awarded to students on the basis of financial need and represents a federal policy to promote equal educational opportunity through greater access to postsecondary educational institutions; it is allocated through Pell Grants (formerly, Basic Educational Opportunity Grants, or BEOGs), Col-

---

1. Some persons and organizations that make financial contributions to a college or university restrict the use of their funds; hence, these funds are termed "restricted." For example, a donor may provide funds specifically for scholarships; thus this aid comes from restricted funds. At many institutions most revenue, like tuition and appropriations, is allocated by the institution's administration and thus is termed "unrestricted." Scholarships provided from these sources come from "unrestricted" funds. The institution's administration determines how these funds are to be spent.

TABLE A

PERCENT DISTRIBUTION OF FORMS OF UNDERGRADUATE STUDENT AID, 1976-77, BY SOURCES OF AID

	All Sources	Institutions	Federal Government	State or Local Government
Total percentage	100.0%	100.0%	100.0%	100.0%
Loans	19.8	2.6	9.0	8.2
Grants and work-study programs	68.3	16.8	37.4	14.1
Employment	10.7	10.7	—	—
Other	1.3	—	—	1.3
Total Dollars (in thousands)	$5,116,100	$1,539,900	$2,368,800	$1,207,400

NOTE: On this table and subsequent tables, dollar amounts are rounded to the nearest $100,000. Because of weighting and rounding, subtotals may not add exactly to totals.

SOURCE: Irene L. Gomberg and Frank J. Atelsek, "The Institutional Share of Undergraduate Financial Assistance, 1976-77," Higher Educational Panel Report, no. 42 (Washington, D.C.: American Council on Education, May 1979), p. 18.

lege Work Study (CWS), National Direct Student Loans (NDSL), and State Student Incentive Grant (SSIG) programs.[2] Other financial aid programs are funded by state governments, private foundations, and other private organizations. Several state and private programs do not award aid primarily on the basis of need but target aid for students with special abilities or selected attributes.

Because the various noninstitutional aid programs have never fully met the financial needs of American students, colleges and universities have drawn on their own funds to augment the aid from these programs. From a historical perspective, it is more precise to say that state aid and federal aid now augment institutional aid programs. In 1976, for example, 2,500 institutions allocated approximately $1.4 billion in student aid—about 30 percent of aid from *all* sources (see table A).

The commitment of colleges and universities to provide substantial financial aid to students prompts several questions. How is institutionally funded student financial aid distributed? Is student financial need the primary criterion for awarding institutional aid? What other criteria are considered? What issues and policies affect the allocation of student aid funds at the federal level, the state level, and the institutional level? How does the outflow of institutionally funded student financial aid affect an institution's financial health?

2. These types of federal financial aid are defined in the appendix.

xiv *Introduction*

This book addresses these questions. It also examines four uses of institutionally funded student financial aid: promoting equal educational opportunity (Chapter 2); recruiting select students (Chapter 3); attracting students in general (Chapter 4); and inducing students to work for the college (Chapter 5). (These distinctions in use are, to some degree, artificial, for some aid is used in all four ways; for example, a needy, academically talented student may be attracted to a college with institutional financial aid partially awarded through a work program. The distinctions are drawn to indicate the potential uses of institutional aid.) Two other chapters discuss policy issues: the first chapter focuses on formulating an institutional financial aid policy, and the sixth chapter deals with the implications of institutional aid for federal aid programs.

I

Institutionally Funded Student Aid and Institutional Policy Issues

The Policies

How much should an institution charge for tuition? How much of its own funds should it budget for student aid? How should it allocate that aid among grants for talented students, grants for needy students, loans, student work programs, and tuition remissions? Among the various types of students—part-time, full-time, in-state, out-of-state, those eligible for federal or state awards, and those ineligible for federal or state awards—how should the institution apportion its aid funds? How should it present these options to students?

The issues implicit in these questions are the basic policy issues facing institutions today. Unfortunately, major changes in these policies are seldom possible. Changes in tuition and the amount of student aid awarded must be incremental to avoid alienating continuing students and to forestall recruiting difficulties. Yet, many large institutions depend heavily on tuition revenue, and an increase in tuition of a single percentage point can mean the gain of hundreds of thousands of dollars. Small institutions may find that small increases in tuition allow them to offer their employees reasonable salary increases.

Few institutions have carefully analyzed their institutionally funded student aid program. Many institutions raise their institutional aid budget 5 percent every year or use a similar rule of thumb when budgeting their funds. During "good" years (when revenue exceeds forecasts), student aid funds may be allocated late in the year from the expected overall surplus. During "bad" years, allocations for institutional student aid may require special pleading. At many institutions, the budgeted figure is not rigidly fixed at the beginning of the year and may depend on student needs and last-minute changes in state and federal program regulations and allocations.

2 Institutional Policy Issues

Institutions package aid in amazingly diverse ways. Cooper's study of California institutions reveals that some institutions award grants to all eligible students and give jobs and loans to students with exceptional need, while others give jobs and loans to all eligible students and award grants to students with exceptional need.[1]

Later chapters will show that institutions may use their institutional student aid for many purposes, including funding students with financial need; recruiting scholars, athletes, and other talented students; and filling work programs. No two institutions formulate financial aid policy or award these funds in the same way. In fact, one value of institutional student aid is that it is flexible: it can be used in various circumstances by various institutions.

The Importance of Refining Institutional Mission

The directive to refine institutional mission, an exhortation often accompanied only by general suggestions about how to do so, has become a cliché among institutional researchers and planners. We have formulated four institutional objectives that must be carefully considered before financial aid policy can be defined. The priorities of these objectives can and probably should change as an institution begins to develop its financial aid policy.

An institution is not likely to revise substantially its financial aid policies solely on the basis of an evaluation of institutional objectives and their priority. At most, institutions should use the evaluation of these priorities as an indication of the *direction* in which financial aid policy should move.

The four objectives that we propose are (1) maximization of revenue (or, for some public institutions, maximization of enrollment); (2) expansion of educational opportunities; (3) achievement of educational excellence; and (4) reduction of operating costs. These four objectives are not necessarily mutually exclusive, but an institution's decision to concentrate on one objective may result in changes in its student financial aid policies that work against the other objectives. For example, an institution's decision to concentrate on achieving educational excellence may weaken its ability to maximize revenue, cut costs, and attract disadvantaged students.

Maximization of revenue requires a greater emphasis on the

---

1. Harlan T. Cooper, "Diversity in College and University Administration of Federal Financial Aid," Ph.D. dissertation, Stanford University, March 1979, p. 83.

marketing of an institution, including an emphasis on making the institution distinct from its competitors in both image and price. An institution should carefully analyze the response of various segments of its market to variations in price. It may find, for example, that the best course of action is to increase tuition while providing more financial aid to the groups most likely to respond to lower *net* tuition.

On the other hand, an institution that wishes to expand educational opportunities to its traditional clientele or to expand opportunities to a new clientele may wish to keep tuition low. These institutions may elect to target financial aid for the most disadvantaged prospective students. Special programs to attract students with financial need will probably require some supplements from institutional funds.

Institutions that wish to achieve greater academic excellence may be less hesitant to raise tuition and may target financial aid for academically talented students from their own funds. This strategy refers to academic excellence in the traditional sense, however, and may not be a viable strategy for institutions concentrating on program excellence for students of lesser abilities.

State appropriation restrictions or other kinds of revenue losses may cause some institutions to neglect the first three objectives and concentrate on reducing operating costs. These institutions may seek to replace institutional money with federal funds to the greatest possible extent. This strategy may be easily pursued by eliminating tuition remissions for students who qualify for federal aid. Replacing institutional funds with federal or state dollars in other programs may not be possible, however, because many institutionally funded aid recipients may not qualify for additional federal or state aid.

An Iterative Pricing Model

Once institutional policy makers have investigated institutional priorities, they may next use an iterative model to determine appropriate tuition rates and student financial aid levels. This iterative model necessitates that the policy makers, who are usually aided by researchers in the admissions office, understand and be able to project sector-by-sector changes in the institution's market. An institution's market consists of persons in appropriate age categories who are potential students. Research by the institution is necessary to determine how many potential students of each type are available.

The iterative pricing model has seven steps (see figure 1.1). *First, the institution must project the potential student market by market*

4 Institutional Policy Issues

segment. The institution must subdivide its market by sex, age (18–25, 26–35, 35 and older, and so forth), interest (vocational, liberal arts), ability (high, low), income (likely financial aid recipients, not likely financial aid recipients), and location (same city, same county, and so forth). Relevant data are available from the Census Bureau, the American Council on Education, and regional planning commissions.

Second, the institution must estimate its segment-by-segment share of the market in relation to other educational institutions and commercial employers. From what segment does the institution draw most of its students? Where has it been most successful against competitors? In its calculation of market share, an institution should include, if possible, not only enrollment at other institutions, but also the number of persons in various segments who are not attending any postsecondary institution. Unfortunately, little data exist to help the institution. Some states, however, do collect and publish enrollment data for all institutions. In addition, the American Council on Education's Policy Analysis Service can compute for any institution its market proportion of part-time and full-time students (both undergraduate and graduate) and the proportion of men and women (both undergraduate and graduate) for the ten years beginning fall 1970. The American Council on Education allows institutions to specify the other institutions they would like included as members of their market.

Third, in formulating an overall marketing plan, an institution must estimate the responsiveness of potential students from each market segment to changes in the institution's net tuition level for that segment. (The net tuititon level for students receiving financial aid will be different from the net tuition level for students not receiving financial aid.[2]) These estimates should be based on a format similar to the following one: x percent increase in net tuition for the market segment composed of middle-income, local residents will result in a drop in market share of less than y percent.

The research on tuition price elasticity, mentioned previously, may be valuable, but it is no substitute for experience. A factor that has often been neglected in these studies is the timing of tuition changes. The importance of timing is apparent in Arizona, where state funding shifts are forcing community colleges to charge tuition. Here prelimi-

2. Each segment's net tuition can be translated into the average amount of financial need that will be unmet. Higher net tuition for some groups may exceed expected contributions, resulting in unmet need for students in that segment.

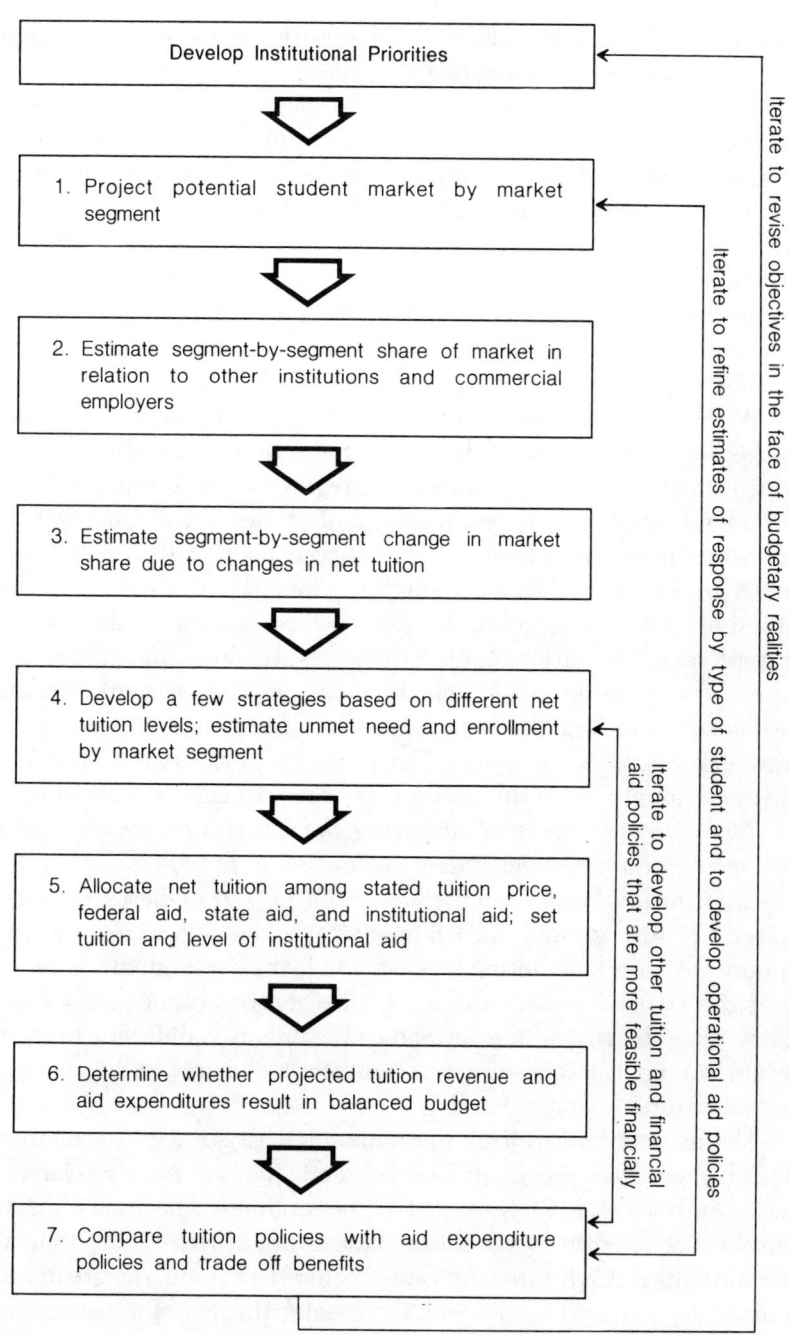

Fig. 1.1. Iterative pricing model

nary assessments of the effect of sizable tuition increases on enrollment indicate that the decrease in enrollment is due less to the amount of the tuition increase than to the amount of time available for students *to plan for* the increase. Community college enrollment initially fell when the new tuition was introduced but, after one or two semesters, returned to normal levels.

The fourth step is to project enrollment levels by segment under three or four possible net tuition strategies. Given a set of net tuition policies for each segment, potential changes in market share can be projected. By knowing the size of each market, the institution should be able to project enrollment.

Within each net tuition strategy, tuition will be different for each market segment because of the usefulness of targeting institutional aid for specific segments. Net tuition strategies may also differ for each market segment because each group of students will qualify for a different amount of federal and state financial aid. A student's state of residence also affects his or her eligibility for aid under state programs; tuition for public institutions, for example, can vary according to state of residence. The various tuition strategies should include alternative approaches to targeting financial aid for special students, students with need, and students who will work for the institution. These strategies should be formulated in response to the four institutional objectives identified in the preliminary stage of this iterative process.

The fifth step requires allocating the net tuition formulated in the strategies among the stated tuition price, federal aid, state aid, and institutional aid. Stated tuition will be the highest net tuition charged to any group (since financial aid can never be a negative amount). Also, a new tuition level should be only marginally different from the level of previous years. Unless the institution establishes a policy whereby the tuition for entering students is different from the tuition for continuing students, significant changes in tuition may result in student dissatisfaction.

At this step, the institution, no matter what strategy for financial aid it has adopted, has made two decisions that are closely related: it has set tuition, and it has estimated the amount of necessary institutional aid. The tuition level affects the amount of federal and state aid that students receive. Obviously, the higher the tuition, the greater the demand for aid, and, in the end, the greater the need for institutional aid to achieve the net tuition assumed in estimating the institution's market share.

Note that in earlier steps of the iterative pricing model, student demand was estimated according to the level of net tuition. At this step, the institution must achieve this net tuition level with some combination of federal, state, and institutional aid and an assumed *gross* tuition level. Institutional aid must make up the difference between the gross price (minus available federal and state aid) and the net price assumed in the calculation of enrollment. The assumptions about enrollment under each strategy can then be used to determine total tuition revenue and total institutional aid expenditure.

The sixth step entails determining whether the projected tuition revenue and aid expenditures result in a balanced budget. Are projected tuition levels high enough and projected institutional aid allotments low enough to allow a balanced budget? Do projections show continued balance? Obviously, a preliminary expenditure budget and budget projection are necessary. Each strategy should result in a different degree of budget balance (or imbalance). In addition, each strategy should allow the institution to pursue its objectives in a slightly different fashion. At this step in the process, the costs of providing an education are compared with the anticipated revenue. If appropriate costs can be calculated in the first step, more realistic strategies can be devised.

The seventh step involves comparing tuition and financial aid policy variations with necessary overall expenditure variations and trading off benefits. At this point, it may be necessary for the institution to return to the fourth step to design three or four more possible net tuition strategies. The use of modeling to compare various policy strategies has been discussed by Dickmeyer, Hopkins, and Massy.[3] Balancing the budget may require higher tuition or lower employee salary raises than planned in the first set of strategies. The student services budget may have to be adjusted to accommodate the amount allocated for institutionally funded student financial aid. Computerization allows such calculations to be made quickly and can provide a prompt overview of the impact of new policies on the overall budget. Such an overview is especially important if a series of trial strategies must be constructed.

Many policy makers may find using so many assumptions too risky to be practical. Although the use of multiple assumptions may

---

3. Nathan Dickmeyer, David S. P. Hopkins, and William F. Massy, "Trades: A Model for Interactive Financial Planning," *NACUBO Business Officer*, March 1978, pp. 22–27.

8 Institutional Policy Issues

seem risky, the administrator should remember that major changes in tuition and financial aid policy may lead to only minor changes in enrollment. As mentioned previously, the most optimistic research has revealed that a $100 *decrease* in tuition will increase enrollment in responsive market segments by only 3 percent.[4]

Institutions with administrators who think in terms of market segments and market shares have a distinct advantage over other institutions: they may *plan* incremental changes in their strategy to approach potential students. The discipline of recognizing all persons in the region as potential students, despite the fact that some groups have not been attracted to the institution in the past, can lead to a set of pricing policies that is most responsive to the needs of these persons and that most reflects the institution's priorities.

Policies for Awarding Aid

Each policy strategy must also include an assumption about how to distribute institutionally funded student aid to students. The first analysis using the iterative pricing model should be based on flexible guidelines for the distribution of aid. Before making awards, however, an institution must have a firm set of rules to ensure that aid applicants are treated equitably and that the institutional budget is maintained.

Most of these strategies are based on an assessment of each student's unmet need. "Unmet need" is difficult to calculate, but it can be approximated using the following procedure. Each student has a standard set of costs—including tuition, room and board, and other expenses—from which an instituiton may deduct federal, state, and private grants for which the student is eligible. The institution may also deduct an amount, based on a standard national formula, that represents contributions of the student and his or her parents.[5] Many institutions also deduct a student's projected earnings for the summer and the academic year. Even the process of assigning students work as part of their financial aid can be handled in a variety of ways.[6] After

---

4. Gregory Jackson and George Weathersby, "Individual Demand for Higher Education: A Review and Analysis of Recent Empirical Studies," *Journal of Higher Education*, November–December 1975, p. 625.

5. On some more sophisticated campuses, students let tuition increases pass with little comment, but when the family contribution formula is adjusted, students immediately occupy the president's office.

6. Some institutions require students to apply for jobs. Other institutions have so few jobs that students compete for them. Still other institutions discourage freshmen from working. Finally, some institutions have insufficient institutional grants, thus making it possible for students with unmet need to avoid some work.

all these contributions are deducted, the remaining education costs must be covered by loans and institutional grants.

Some institutions that can afford sizable institutional grants have devised formulas for estimating the amount of money students can be expected to borrow. These institutions then try to make up, with institutionally funded loans, the difference between costs to the student and grant aid. In doing so, they must consider the ethical question of the maximum reasonable amount of debt that a student should have incurred upon leaving college. This maximum amount depends, to some extent, on what these students can expect to earn upon graduation. Will most of them go on to graduate school and more debt? How long may students take to pay their debt? What percentage of income in the form of loan repayments can be expected from students after graduation?

Each institution must answer these questions before setting loan policies. Institutions that avoid addressing these policy questions risk dissatisfaction among their graduates. They may also inadvertently encourage attrition by creating greater and greater financial pressure for their students, who may conclude that the delay in entering the job market may no longer be worth the additional education or the degree.

On the other hand, some institutions may not be using loans to the degree they reasonably might. Some institutions may be diverting funds that could have been used for improving academic programs and appropriating these for institutionally funded grants. A decline in the quality and availability of academic programs may ensue, with a resulting drop in enrollment. Such effects would be, of course, contrary to the purpose of the program.

Loans are less of a burden than they sometimes appear to be, however. The fact that the inflation rate is currently so high means that the dollars later used for loan repayments will be cheaper than current dollars. Moreover, interest expense can be deducted from income for tax purposes. Educating students about the advantages of loans can, however, be difficult.

From the institution's perspective, loans require the same outflow of cash as grants. Because of inflation, delays in collection, and the number of uncollectible accounts, loan repayments cannot be expected to cover fully the costs of future loan programs. Students and aid officers also seem to look on loans with disfavor. As a result, loans are rarely used as tools for recruiting academically talented students. Data from the Cooperative Institutional Research Program show that

10 Institutional Policy Issues

TABLE 1.1

PERCENT DISTRIBUTION OF INSTITUTIONAL GRANTS AND LOANS TO FRESHMEN, DISTRIBUTED ACCORDING TO HIGH SCHOOL GRADES

Grades	Grant Only	Loan Only	Loan and Grant	Total of All Packages
A or A+	23.4%	7.6%	17.5%	20.0%
A−	20.9	11.0	17.3	18.8
B+	22.9	22.4	21.6	22.7
B	18.2	27.4	21.7	20.2
B−	6.9	12.1	9.0	8.1
C+	4.8	12.4	7.6	6.4
C	2.6	6.6	4.7	3.7
D	0.2	0.4	0.5	0.2
Total %	100.0	100.0	100.0	100.0

SOURCE: Unpublished 1978 analysis of 1976 Cooperative Institutional Research Program data, Policy Analysis Service, American Council on Education.

many institutions prefer to give grants to students with good high school grade averages and to give loans to lower achievers. Almost 70 percent of all institutional grants were distributed to freshmen whose high school grade average was a *B* or higher; 23 percent of all grants were distributed to freshmen with *A* or *A+* averages. On the other hand, only 8 percent of all institutional loans were distributed to freshmen who had *A* or *A+* grades in high school; 41 percent of the loan recipients had high school grade averages of *B* or higher. The majority of college loans and grant-loan packages, however, went to students with high school grades in the *B+* to *B-* range. Thus, financial aid policy makers should recognize the current belief that loans cannot be used to attract academically talented students (see table 1.1).

A reasonable loan policy might stipulate, as part of the "self help" student aid package component, that students will not be expected to accumulate more debt than they could repay at the rate of 5 percent of gross expected monthly income in ten years (the amount of allowable indebtedness could be based on the average income of recent graduates). Furthermore, since students who complete degree programs have a better chance of earning more money and may feel less inclined to default on loan payments than students who do not, freshmen ought to be awarded more institutionally funded grants and fewer institutionally funded loans than seniors.

After the institution has calculated unmet need for each student and developed policies governing student loan burdens, it must devise policies to guide the awarding of institutional funds. Below are examples of rules governing the allocation of institutionally funded student aid.

1. An institution that faces competition from well-known, more prestigious institutions and that wishes to improve the quality of its program and its reputation may use financial aid to attract the best students while maintaining the diversity of the student body. To this end, it may initially set aside institutional funds sufficient for affirmative action student aid grants and student aid grants to foreign students. Funds can then be earmarked for the continuation of scholarships for sophomores and upperclassmen who were awarded grants as freshmen. Freshmen applicants can then be ranked according to their "desirability" (the most important factor might be the applicant's entering test score). The institution might award each student, beginning with those in the top rank, an institutional grant sufficient to cover any financial need not met by state, federal, or private sources (the usual contribution of the parents is still expected, although the loan component is kept to a minimum).

The limited amount of institutionally funded aid, however, usually prevents the institution from making institutional awards to all applicants. Thus, although applicants with the lowest ranking may be acceptable to the institution, they may not receive institutional grants (beyond the award of federal, state, and private grants) to cover any unmet need. This policy of awarding grants that cover the full need of the top applicants and of not meeting need for the remainder of the applicants is designed to improve an institution's ability to attract the most highly qualified applicants.

2. Some institutions may find that their applicants are relatively homogeneous with respect to quality and may not wish to become competitive with more selective institutions. Yet these institutions may have the same problem as the institution mentioned above—insufficient funds to award to all applicants scholarships covering full need. These colleges and universities may thus seek to spread their shortfall of institutionally funded student aid equally among students. If only 80 percent of the needed funds is available, then the funds will be used to fill an equal percentage—only 80 percent—of each student's unmet need.

3. Some institutions have been able to increase tuition without losing enrollment and have been able to sustain (to date, at least) a policy meeting all the unmet need of all students with institutionally

funded grants. These institutions usually are well endowed and receive strong private support.

4. Other institutions may not have sufficient funds for meeting full unmet need with institutional grants (for example, they may have "invested" more funds in academic programs), and yet they may not be willing to spread the shortfall evenly among students. One policy variation involves using most of the available funds to fund fully the students with the largest unmet need. These institutions would rather fund $990 of student X's $1000 need and nothing of student Y's $100 need than fund an equal percentage (for example, 90 percent) of each student's need. Under this system, students with the largest need get preferential access to institutional money.

5. Another variation of the equal percentage rule requires that a certain amount each student's need be funded by grants and that a certain amount be funded by loans and student work programs. For example, two-thirds of each student's need could be funded by grants and one-third by loans and student work programs. The percentages vary somewhat according to the availability of grants, but institutional funds are used as much as possible to maintain the percentages from year to year. This system greatly eases the packaging process but may put a large loan burden on students with great need. The system will work best at low-tuition institutions, like community colleges, where the variation in unmet need is not great.

6. At some institutions the students' income level is not only low but uniformly low. These institutions do not award institutional aid because 95 percent of their students would qualify and its only effect would be to necessitate higher tuition. At institutions with negligible institutional student aid and negligible contributions from parents, tuition levels are directly tied to state and federal aid allocation policies. When Pell Grants were cut by $50 per student in 1979–80, one of these institutions rescinded a tuition increase—it knew its students could not afford an increase in tuition as well as a decrease in grant money.

7. Another policy variation sets up no guidelines for the distribution of institutionally funded aid, allowing the financial aid officer to disburse the funds at his or her discretion. Although this policy fosters favoritism and encourages students to cultivate the financial aid officer, most institutions that use this policy have limited institutional aid funds, and the financial aid officer is in the best position to assess true emergencies.

These sample policies demonstrate some financial aid allocation methods that institutions have used to help meet larger objectives. Many institutions cannot meet the full financial needs of their students. The following section discusses some alternatives for students with unmet financial need.

Unmet Need

Boston College has done a study of the methods students use to meet any remaining need after tapping the resources discussed above.[7] A sample of 148 students was divided into two groups: on-campus residents and commuters. Students residing on campus made up their unmet need in the following way: 36 percent of the unmet need was funded by guaranteed insured loans; 34 percent was funded by contributions from parents in excess of the standard formula amount; 20 percent was funded by the liquidation of student assets in excess of amount allotted by the standard financial aid formula; and 10 percent was funded by money the students earned by working more than was expected during the summer or by taking jobs apart from work-study employment during the academic year. None of the resident students was able to make up any significant amount of the unmet need by reducing their costs below those calculated by the financial aid office as part of the student budget.

Commuter students showed a slightly different profile. Only 7 percent of their unmet need was funded by contributions from parents in excess of the standard formula amount. Thirty-seven percent was funded by money the students earned by working more than was expected during the summer or by taking jobs apart from work-study employment during the academic year; 25 percent was funded by the liquidation of student assets; 25 percent was funded by guaranteed insured loans; and 6 percent was funded by the reduction of student costs below those calculated for the student budget.

This small sample from one college does not provide a national profile, it does give an idea of the methods students use to make up the difference between costs and available aid. Although most of these students turned to work to supplement their needs, most of the unmet need itself (in terms of total dollars) was funded by loans.

The President's Involvement

At many institutions, the president is only minimally involved in making decisions about student financial aid. Understanding the

---

7. J. Stephen Collins, John J. Maguire, and Robert M. Turner, "Unmet Need: How the Gap Is Filled," *The Journal of Student Financial Aid*, May 1979, pp. 9–15.

details of federal student aid programs requires technical training far beyond that of most presidents. As a result, top-level college and university administrators have avoided the whole area of financial aid policy making.

At one time, student financial aid programs were small enough to justify casual attention. Now, however, the dollar volume that the financial aid office handles often easily exceeds the dollar volume that the development office handles. Yet the president is almost always more involved in development than in financial aid policy making.

As a result, financial aid policy is made in a vacuum and is not coordinated with other institutional policies. Financial aid policies directly affect institutional growth, marketing, and even academic policies and planning. For example, a decision to lower the amount of institutional aid available and to increase the amount of unmet financial need may run contrary to the institution's marketing design. The overall coordination of these planning areas usually requires a greater degree of presidential involvement than presently exists. Such coordination also dictates that the president and his or her team exercise greater authority in setting financial aid policies.

The president's involvement is especially critical in the following areas:

1. *Setting the tuition rate for the next year.* This decision also involves setting special rates for particular groups of students.

2. *Deciding the total amount of institutional funds to be made available as grants to students.* This decision cannot be made without simultaneously deciding tuition levels and funds needed for other institutional expenditures. For example, the amount of institutional funds available for faculty salaries may be increased or decreased depending on the amount budgeted for student grants. In other words, faculty salaries may be traded off against student grants. The institution must assess the benefits of putting equal amounts of money into either category and of trading off the benefits that accrue. The institution must decide what will be worth more in the long run—the potential improvement of the faculty or the improved enrollment drawn with extra aid funds?

3. *Structuring the aid to be awarded.* Dividing funds among grants, student work programs, and loans as well as among different types of students requires a more detailed set of policies. These policies include decisions about work responsibilities for students with financial need, maximum loan amounts that ethically should be required of

Institutional Policy Issues 15

students, and expectations about how students will make up any unmet need.

4. *Special uses of aid.* The institution must develop policies that direct the aid into institutional programs for marketing, affirmative action, student work programs, or program development (academic programs or athletics, for example).

The policy areas described here are crucial to the continued strength of an institution. Each policy must reflect the institution's overall mission and its distinctive character. In turn, each can have a major effect on the institution's development. The president must be directly involved in these decisions and must work closely with the financial aid officer and planning offices in order to understand the implications of each policy.

II

Institutionally Funded Student Aid and Equal Educational Opportunity

Throughout their history, institutions of higher education in America have awarded grants to students with financial need. Recently, federal student aid policy has been directed at promoting equal educational opportunity for persons who face barriers to higher education. Institutional funds are still an important complement to federal programs in achieving this goal. The Higher Education Act of 1965 marked the first authorization of federal funds to assist low-income undergraduate students when college costs might prevent them from attending college. The Education Amendments of 1972 furthered the cause of equal opportunity by establishing Basic Educational Opportunity Grants (BEOGs, now Pell Grants), which, unlike the grants authorized in 1965, were to be given directly to students. Pell Grants are awarded on the basis of a formula that takes into account the income and assets of the student and his or her parents as well as college costs. The BEOG program, which provides need-based subsidies directly to students, lies at the heart of current federal aid policy.

The states have, in general, also adopted policies that make higher education more widely available. Most states have fostered access to higher education by keeping tuition at public institutions low and by expanding the number of state-financed educational facilities.[1] Many state legislatures have promoted college opportunities for low-income persons by authorizing programs of scholarships, loans, and other forms of need-based student aid. Well-funded

---

1. Kenneth M. Deitch, "Financial Aid: A Resource for Improving Educational Opportunities" (Washington, D.C.: Sloan Commission on Government and Higher Education, March 1978), p. 14.

assistance programs, however, are concentrated in just a few states.

Colleges and universities initiated need-based grants and remain a major force in the movement for greater equity of educational opportunity. In 1976–77, need-based grant aid drawn from institutional resources totaled $477 million; this amount constituted 34 percent of all institutionally funded aid and 9.3 percent of aid from institutional and public sources in 1976–77. Loan and employment aid is often also awarded on a need basis; such aid from institutional resources totals another $680 million, or 14 percent of total assistance available.[2]

Access, Choice, and Maintenance of Aid

Equal educational opportunity can be achieved through a combination of access, reasonable choice, and maintenance of aid. *Access* and *choice* may be defined in several ways. The National Commission on the Financing of Postsecondary Education defines *access* as the opportunity for a person to "enroll in some form of postsecondary education"; it defines *choice* as the opportunity for a person to choose among institutions "appropriate to that person's needs, capability, and motivation."[3] The National Association of College and University Business Officers interprets *access* as "the elimination of all nonacademic barriers that prevent a student from attending an institution of higher education"; it interprets *choice* as the opportunity for a student to attend the best possible institution with respect to "his or her academic qualifications and motivation."[4] Maintenance of aid, the third factor in ensuring equal educational opportunity, involves providing aid to a student not only to begin a college education but also to pursue that education as long as he or she is qualified and motivated.

The goals of access, choice, and maintenance of aid imply a "leveling up" or raising of the rates of low-income persons who have traditionally faced barriers to postsecondary education but who are

---

2. Irene L. Gomberg and Frank J. Atelsek, "The Institutional Share of Undergraduate Financial Assistance, 1976–77," Higher Education Panel Report no. 42 (Washington, D.C.: American Council on Education, May 1979), pp. 6–7.

3. National Commission on the Financing of Postsecondary Education, *Financing Postsecondary Education in the United States* (Washington, D.C.: U.S. Government Printing Office, December 1973), p. 55.

4. National Association of College and University Business Officers, *Management of Student Aid* (Washington, D.C.: NACUBO, 1980), p. 6.

now surmounting these barriers. On this basis, complete access will be achieved when rates of participation in postsecondary education are the same for populations that differ according to income, race, ethnicity, sex, and residence.

Finances, however, are not the only barrier to complete access. Before complete access is possible, educational and development opportunities for children and adolescents must be expanded. Complete choice will be achieved when attendance rates for these groups do not vary among institutions categorized by selectivity or cost of attendance. Maintenance of aid occurs when the rates of aid for sophomores, juniors, and seniors keep pace with the rates of aid for freshmen.

Although access and choice were once deemed complementary, they now connote rival policy objectives. Policies promoting access are often thought to favor low-tuition public institutions, whereas policies favoring choice seem to benefit private institutions. With the projecteddecline in the pool of students of traditional college age, the rival policies of access and choice will, in the future, have a direct bearing on the competition among institutions to enroll qualified students.[5] Subsidies appropriated for the promotion of access will help low-tuition public institutions attract students. On the other hand, funds earmarked for the promotion of choice will help private institutions compete for students. Important policy deliberations rest on balancing considerations of access and choice without unduly burdening either public or private institutions.

The Role of Institutionally Funded Student Aid

Need-based institutionally funded grants provided by colleges and universities in 1976–77 represented almost one-tenth of all student aid available in that year. These grants were thus an important factor in promoting equal educational opportunity. When low-tuition colleges and universities, generally in the public sector, award relatively large amounts of need-based financial aid from institutional funds, they promote access to institutionally funded student aid by reducing student costs to negligible amounts. When more expensive institutions, both public and private, award large amounts of need-based financial aid from institutional funds, institutionally funded student aid may be said to promote both access and choice. Clearly, in-

---

5. Deitch, p. 5.

Equal Educational Opportunity 19

stitutionally funded student aid awarded by public colleges also encourages choice.

An American Council on Education survey shows the degree to which institutionally funded aid is used to promote equal opportunity by reducing the cost of attending institutions with high tuition. During the 1976–77 academic year, private institutions disbursed more than twice the amount of need-based institutionally funded grants ($359 million) than did public colleges and universities ($118 million), despite the fact that public institutions enrolled three times the number of students (see table 2.1). Students attending private institutions, however, had to pay for tuition costs that were, on the average, five times as great. Thus, students attending private colleges needed more institutional aid to compensate for the higher costs of these institutions. This aid amounted to $204 in institutional scholarship, loan, and work funds for every full-time student enrolled in a private institution in 1976.

TABLE 2.1

PERCENT AND DOLLAR DISTRIBUTION OF FORMS OF INSTITUTIONALLY FUNDED UNDERGRADUATE AID, 1976–77, BY INSTITUTIONAL CONTROL

	Private Institutions		Public Institutions	
	Amount	%	Amount	%
Need-based awards	$359,150,000	50.0%	$118,470,000	17.2%
Targeted awards	112,770,000	15.7	121,230,000	17.6
Tuition remissions	80,450,000	11.2	22,730,000	3.3
Employment funds	150,840,000	21.0	338,139,000	57.8
Total	718,300,000	100.0	688,800,000	100.0

SOURCE: Irene L. Gomberg and Frank J. Atelsek, "The Institutional Share of Undergraduate Financial Assistance, 1976–77," Higher Education Panel Report no. 42 (Washington, D.C.: American Council on Education, May 1979), p. 18.

For private institutions, the chief source of need-based awards from unrestricted general funds is tuition; for public institutions, the chief source is appropriations. Contrasting the 1976–77 figures for private and public institutions reveals that private colleges and universities provided $255 million in need-based grants from unrestricted funds, the equivalent of $150 for each of the 1.76 million full-time students enrolled in private institutions in 1976–77.[6] In other words, each private institution used $150 from each tuition charge to subsidize students with financial need. This figure represents 6.2 percent of the average yearly tuition for private institutions in 1976. The distribution among tuition payers varied, of course, depending on the proportion of students assisted. The comparable figure for public institutions was $88 million in institutional funds for need-based grants—$17.66 per full-time student and 3.7 percent of the average tuition payment of $474. The average grant, even as a proportion of the average tuition, is smaller in public institutions.

Private institutions gave higher priority to need-based awards than to targeted awards, tuition remissions, and employment funds (see table 2.1). Half the private institutions' institutionally funded aid went to need-based awards, while 17.2 percent of the public institutions' institutionally funded aid went to need-based awards.

Table 2.1 also shows that public colleges and universities allocated almost 58 percent of their institutionally funded student aid for employment funds. Some of these funds, although not identified as such, probably served a need-based role. The fact that this aid does not come from federally related funds (except for the federal matching portions) indicates that many students receiving these funds are not defined as needy. Yet since these students work, they may *perceive*

TABLE 2.2

PERCENT DISTRIBUTION OF INSTITUTIONALLY FUNDED NEED-BASED, MERIT, AND ATHLETIC GRANTS, 1976–77, BY INSTITUTIONAL TYPE AND CONTROL

Public Institutions	Institutionally Funded Grants		
	Need-based	Merit	Athletic
Universities	16.9%	7.7%	9.3%
Four-year colleges	17.8	10.0	9.7
Two-year colleges	17.3	8.4	5.8
Private Institutions			
Universities	55.8	5.2	7.6
Four-year colleges	47.1	11.5	5.7

SOURCE: Irene L. Gomberg and Frank J. Atelsek, "The Institutional Share of Undergraduate Financial Assistance, 1976–77," Higher Education Panel Report no. 42 (Washington, D.C.: American Council on Education, May 1979), p. 19.

6. Gomberg and Atelsek, p. 18.

themselves as needy. Hence, public institutions are probably channeling more than 17 percent of their institutionally funded student aid into need-related aid programs. Unfortunately, the exact amount of additional need-based aid cannot be determined.

Furthermore, this trend did not vary greatly by institutional type. The data from the American Council on Education reveal that private universities and four-year colleges allocated approximately 50 percent of their institutionally funded grants on the basis of need. Public institutions distributed 16.9 percent; four-year colleges distributed 17.8 percent; and two-year colleges distributed 17.3 percent (see table 2.2).

TABLE 2.3

PERCENT DISTRIBUTION OF INSTITUTIONALLY FUNDED UNDERGRADUATE GRANTS, 1978-79, BY INSTITUTIONAL TYPE AND CONTROL AND BY TUITION LEVEL

		Institutionally Funded Grants	
Private Institutions	Tuition	Need-based	Ability-based
Four year	>$2500	13.7%	5.4%
Four year	<$2500	3.2	8.5
Two year	>$1200	10.5	9.6
Two year	<$1200	0.6	0.2
Public Institutions			
Four year	>$ 700	4.8	4.3
Four year	<$ 700	2.6	1.3
Two year	>$ 300	0.3	1.0
Two year	<$ 300	0.0	0.3

SOURCE: Based on Patricia A. Smith, Paula R. Knepper, Janet P. Jackley, Cathy Henderson, "Financing Undergraduate Education in 1978-79," Policy Analysis Service (Washington, D.C.: American Council on Education, June 1980), pp. 21-27.

Data generated by an Applied Management Sciences (AMS) study of campus-based grant programs funded by the U.S. Department of Education and analyzed by the American Council on Education reveal that during the 1978-79 academic year the distribution of institutionally funded grants varied markedly by tuition level.

The AMS survey used in table 2.3 is able to show the proportion of students receiving particular kinds of institutional aid because the table is based on individual student aid packaging data rather than aggregate institutional data, on which the American Council on

TABLE 2.4

AVERAGE AMOUNT OF UNDERGRADUATE INSTITUTIONALLY FUNDED STUDENT AID (IFSA), TUITION, FEES, ROOM AND BOARD, 1976-77, BY CATEGORY OF INSTITUTION

Category of Institution	IFSA (grants and employment) Per Undergraduate	Total Tuition, Room and Board	Percentage Covered by IFSA	Total Tuition, Room and Board Less IFSA	Tuition and Fees Only	Percentage Covered by IFSA
Total	$ 627	$2,307	27%	$1,680	$ 958	65%
Public Institutions						
Universities	750	2,055	36	1,305	676	111
Four-year colleges	398	1,797	22	1,393	528	75
Two-year colleges	141	1,488	9	1,347	274	51
Total	412	1,790	23	1,378	474	87
Private Institutions						
Universities	1,676	4,847	35	3,171	3,142	53
Four-year colleges	1,107	3,562	31	2,455	2,189	51
Two-year colleges[a]	511	2,905	18	2,394	1,517	34
Total	1,227	3,856	32	2,629	2,408	51

NOTE: [a] Data from private two-year colleges should be used with caution and only in conjunction with their standard errors as shown in Appendix Table C-6 of HEP Report no. 42.

SOURCES: Data from Higher Education Panel Report no. 42 (Washington, D.C.: American Council on Education, May 1979); Leo Eidens, National Center for Education Statistics; and Cathy Henderson, American Council on Education.

Education–Higher Education Panel (HEP) survey is based.[7] In terms of the number of grants to undergraduates, the private institutions with high tuition, not surprisingly, exceed other types of institutions in distributing need-based awards.

With the exception of two-year institutions with low tuition, public colleges awarded institutional aid to 5 to 10 percent of their students, whereas private institutions awarded institutional aid to 16 to 21 percent of their students. Private institutions awarded institutional aid to two to three times more students than did public institutions.

Whether under public or private control, high-tuition institutions of the same type (i.e., two-year institutions as opposed to four-year institutions) were more likely to award need-based aid. Table 2.3 also shows that ability-based aid was more predominant in private institutions but was not related to tuition levels.

The average proportion of total tuition and room and board accounted for by institutionally funded grants and employment is shown in the HEP data in table 2.4. Institutional grants and employment aid at private institutions averaged 32 percent of tuition and room and board costs, compared with 27 percent at public institutions. Yet the average amount of costs not covered by institutional aid was $2,629 for private institutions, compared with $1,680 for public institutions. This analysis indicates that the high level of institutional awards made by private institutions is related to high tuition and that

TABLE 2.5

NUMBER OF INSTITUTIONAL GRANTS AND TUITION REMISSIONS, AS A PERCENTAGE OF GRANTS AWARDED TO FRESHMEN, 1978–79, BY YEAR IN SCHOOL

Form of Grant Aid	Freshman	Sophomore	Junior	Senior
Need-based	100.0%	88.5%	65.3%	58.9%
Ability-based	100.0	69.5	56.4	56.3
Tuition remission	100.0	72.8	34.1	20.9

SOURCE: Patricia A. Smith, Paula R. Knepper, Janet P. Jackley, and Cathy Henderson, "Financing Undergraduate Education in 1978–79," Policy Analysis Service (Washington, D.C.: American Council on Education, June 1980).

7. Note that the AMS figures do not include employment or loans, two important forms of institutional aid. These data are included in the HEP aggregates, and this inclusion partially accounts for the difference in magnitude of the HEP and AMS data. Also, the HEP data use full-time equivalent students in the denominator in "proportion of undergraduates" calculations; AMS uses headcount data.

TABLE 2.6

ENROLLMENT IN HIGHER EDUCATION FOR EACH CLASS, AS A PERCENTAGE OF FRESHMEN, 1978-79, BY YEAR IN SCHOOL

Enrollment Figures	Freshman	Sophomore	Junior	Senior
Total	100.0%	48.8%	28.1%	27.8%
FTE	120.0	40.1	38.8	36.2

SOURCE: National Center for Education Statistics, "Fall Enrollment in Higher Education" (Washington, D.C.: U.S. Government Printing Office, 1979).

TABLE 2.7

PERCENT DISTRIBUTION OF DEPENDENT UNDERGRADUATE STUDENT AID RECIPIENTS, BY UNADJUSTED GROSS FAMILY INCOME AND SOURCE OF AID, 1976-77

Status and Family Income	Recipients of OE Aid Programs	Recipients of Any Institutional Aid	Recipients of Institutional Aid Only
Total number	1,394,000	1,820,000	462,300
Total percentage	100%	100%	100%
Dependent undergraduates, by unadjusted gross family income			
Less than $7,500	46	34	22
$ 7,500-11,999	25	22	18
$12,000-14,999	17	10	19
$15,000 or more	12	23	41

SOURCE: Based on Irene L. Gomberg and Frank J. Atelsek, "The Institutional Share of Undergraduate Financial Assistance, 1976-77," Higher Education Panel Report no. 42 (Washington, D.C.: American Council on Education, May 1979).

even after the higher awards are made, the level of student support needed from other sources is higher than at public institutions.

With respect to maintaining aid, AMS data and enrollment data from the National Center for Education Statistics (NCES) reveal that, in the aggregate, the number of institutionally funded grants more than kept pace with the number of freshmen, sophomores, juniors, and seniors (see table 2.5). According to table 2.6, institutions awarded a greater percentage of institutionally funded student aid grants to sophomores, juniors, and seniors in relation to the percentage of sophomores, juniors, and seniors enrolled in postsecondary education. Thus, institutions maintained their offers of institutionally funded grant aid to enable students to complete their education.

Moreover, the percentage of institutionally funded grants outpaced the percentage of students enrolled in each class (see table 2.6).

TABLE 2.8

PERCENT DISTRIBUTION OF DEPENDENT UNDERGRADUATE STUDENT AID RECIPIENTS, BY UNADJUSTED GROSS FAMILY INCOME, SOURCE OF AID, AND CONTROL, 1976-77

Status and Family Income	Recipients of OE Aid Programs	Recipients of Any Institutional Aid	Recipients of Institutional Aid Only
Public Institutions			
Total number	961,400	1,268,400	327,100
Total percentage	100%	100%	100%
Dependent undergraduates, by unadjusted gross family income			
Less than $7,500	52	40	25
$ 7,500-11,999	25	24	22
$12,000-14,999	15	20	22
$15,000 or more	8	16	32
Private Institutions			
Total number	432,900	552,000	135,100
Total percentage	100%	100%	100%
Dependent undergraduates, by unadjusted gross family income			
Less than $7,500	32	20	15
$ 7,500-11,999	25	19	9
$12,000-14,999	20	20	13
$15,000 or more	23	41	63

SOURCE: Based on Irene L. Gomberg and Frank J. Atelsek, "The Institutional Share of Undergraduate Financial Assistance, 1976-77," Higher Education Panel Report no. 42 (Washington, D.C.: American Council on Education, May 1979), p. 26.

These data suggest that these awards may have been instrumental in suppressing the dropout rates of aid recipients. On the other hand, institutionally funded student aid may be awarded at a higher rate to sophomores and upperclassmen because they have proven their ability to stay in school. Furthermore, these students may be most likely to have financial difficulty, for the burden of paying for college accumulates through the student's academic career.

Distribution of Institutionally Funded Student Aid by Family Income

Family income is the most important variable in determining financial need. Thus, an examination of the role of institutionally funded student aid in promoting educational opportunity should include a brief look at the distribution of such aid by student family income.

In 1976–77, 88 percent of aid funded by the Office of Education (OE) and allocated for students went to those whose family income was less than $15,000, as indicated in table 2.7. The institution was somewhat more likely to be the source of aid for students with family incomes exceeding $15,000. One quarter of the students receiving any institutional aid came from families earning more than $15,000. Nationally, this trend was most pronounced at private institutions, where 41 percent of the recipients of any institutional aid and 63 percent of the recipients of *only* institutional aid (and no other form of aid) had family incomes exceeding $15,000 (see table 2.8).

Of those students who received only institutionally funded student aid, 60 percent came from income groups that are supposedly eligible for federal and for most state aid. For these students, the institutions themselves are the only source of aid. Many of these students may be foreign; many may attend less than half time and thus be ineligible for federal aid. Institutionally funded student aid, however, clearly fills a gap not addressed by standardized federal and state programs.

On the whole, however, students from middle-income families were better served by institutionally funded student aid than by aid from federal programs, as is shown in data gathered by the Cooperative Institutional Research Program,[8] the American Council on Education, and the Higher Education Research Laboratory at UCLA. During the 1976–77 academic year, 48.6 percent of institutionally funded grants went to freshmen whose family income was above $15,000, while only 18.4 percent of BEOGs and 17.0 percent of SEOGs went to students whose family income was above $15,000 (see table 2.9). In the same vein, AMS data for the 1977–78 academic year (see table 2.10) show that more than half the institutionally funded grants went to students in the middle-income bracket (above $15,000).

According to table 2.10, 155,800 grants (28.5 percent) went to students whose family income exceeded $25,000 per annum; an additional 138,300 grants (25.3 percent) went to students whose family income was in the $18,000–$24,000 bracket. On the other

---

8. The Cooperative Institutional Research Program (CIRP) is a national longitudinal study of the American higher education system. Established in 1966 by the American Council on Education, CIRP is now the largest ongoing empirical study of American higher education. It gathers data on more than 600 institutions, 100,000 faculty members, and 3.0 million students.

TABLE 2.9

PERCENT DISTRIBUTION OF STUDENT AID AWARDS TO FIRST-TIME, FULL-TIME FRESHMEN, BY LEVEL OF FAMILY INCOME, 1976-77

Student Aid Program	Number of Awards[a]	Less than $6,000	$6,000–$9,999	$10,000–$12,499	$12,500–$14,999	$15,000–$19,999	$20,000–$24,999	$25,000 and over	Total	Family Income Above $15,000
BEOG	246,015	30.5%[b]	24.7%	15.7%	10.7%	9.1%	4.6%	4.7%	100.0%	18.4
SEOG	64,851	31.0	24.1	16.4	11.5	10.1	3.9	3.0	100.0	17.0
CWS	121,030	21.4	18.9	15.5	13.9	16.2	7.8	6.3	100.0	30.3
NDSL	81,511	17.8	18.0	16.3	15.6	18.9	8.4	5.0	100.0	32.3
GSL	70,125	10.8	12.1	12.6	14.3	21.1	14.3	14.8	100.0	50.2
State scholarship or grant	148,724	15.3	17.2	16.0	15.1	18.5	9.8	8.1	100.0	36.4
Institutionally funded grant	131,577	11.1	12.8	13.4	14.2	20.3	13.5	14.8	100.1	48.6
Other private grant	90,371	9.8	11.8	12.6	13.8	19.2	14.7	18.0	99.9	51.9
Institutional loan	40,027	17.1	15.3	14.2	15.2	18.6	11.2	8.5	100.1	38.3
All other loans	38,295	7.9	10.2	12.3	13.6	21.6	15.9	18.6	100.1	56.1
Personal G. I. benefits	12,314	24.3	16.0	16.4	11.6	12.4	8.5	10.8	100.0	31.7
Social security	72,481	29.0	21.9	14.4	10.5	9.1	5.9	9.2	100.0	24.2
Students receiving aid from at least one of the above programs (unduplicated count)	554,350	16.9	15.7	13.6	12.9	16.7	11.1	13.0	99.9	40.8
Percentage of students in each income category	—	10.7	10.9	11.1	12.2	17.2	13.6	24.3	100.0	55.1

NOTE: Detailed distributions of these programs by family income and cost of institution attended are available from Policy Analysis Service, American Council on Education.

[a] This data on number of awards should be interpreted one program at a time. Because some students receive a package of aid, the number of aided students is smaller than the total awards distributed.

[b] To read, 30.5 percent of the total BEOG awards received by first-time, full-time freshmen (246,015) went to students with a gross family income of less than $6,000.

SOURCE: Based on Policy Analysis Service data, American Council on Education.

TABLE 2.10

DISTRIBUTION OF STUDENT AID AWARDS, BY FAMILY INCOME

Type of Aid	Less than $6,000	$6,000–$11,999	$12,000–$17,999	$18,000–$24,999	$25,000 or more	Total*
Institutionally funded and private grants	49,400 (9.0%)	85,400 (15.6%)	117,800 (21.6%)	138,300 (25.3%)	155,800 (28.5%)	546,600 (100.0%)
BEOG	249,700 (28.3)	308,100 (34.9)	220,600 (25.0)	75,600 (8.6)	28,700 (3.3)	882,800 (100.0)
SEOG	64,600 (24.6)	82,100 (31.3)	75,800 (28.9)	29,000 (11.0)	11,300 (4.3)	262,700 (100.0)
CWS	76,800 (17.9)	117,400 (27.4)	113,900 (26.6)	74,600 (17.4)	45,500 (10.6)	428,000 (100.0)
GSL	29,900 (6.5)	40,500 (11.4)	95,600 (26.9)	93,400 (26.3)	102,500 (28.9)	355,000 (100.0)
NDSL	61,400 (13.5)	113,000 (24.9)	137,900 (30.3)	99,200 (21.8)	42,900 (9.4)	454,500 (100.0)

SOURCE: Policy Analysis Service, American Council on Education, May 1980; based on student-reported data from the FY78–79 study of program management procedures in the Campus-Based and Basic Grant Programs, conducted by Applied Management Sciences for the Office of Evaluation and Dissemination of USCE under contract number OE-300-78-0498. The FY78–79 study sample is representative of all undergraduate students enrolled half-time or more.

*Totals reduced by the approximately 20 percent of students whose family incomes were undetermined.

hand, this table confirms that institutions also provide funds to the neediest students—one quarter of their awards go to students whose family income is below $12,000.

The fact that a significant amount of institutionally funded aid went to middle-income students does not mean that this aid was not need-based. According to a College Board publication prepared by Hansen and Gladieus, 55 percent of families filing the College Scholarship Service (CSS) forms for student aid in 1977–78 had incomes between $12,000 and $35,000 and showed measured need, especially at more expensive colleges.[9] In fact, the Middle Income Student Assistance Act (MISAA) was legislated in response to the financial needs of college students whose family income was above the poverty level. Prior to the passage of MISAA, Congress was concerned that middle-income families were receiving too little financial assistance given their proportionate ability to pay.[10] Many middle-income

9. Janet S. Hansen and Lawrence E. Gladieus, *Middle-Income Students: A New Target for Federal Aid?* (New York: College Entrance Examination Board, 1978), p. 7.

10. See Hansen and Gladieux. See also Michael S. McPherson, *Public Policy and Private Higher Education*, eds. David W. Breneman and Chester E. Finn, Jr. (Washington, D.C.: The Brookings Institution, 1978).

families were facing significant financial burdens by sending their children to their chosen college, primarily because of wide variations in college costs but also because of many other factors, including the so-called sibling-overlap problem.

Because of the existence of unmet financial need for many middle-income students, private institutions have allocated much of their institutionally funded student aid to these students. Private institutions have thus augmented federal aid programs, which were designed to assist needy students from lower-income families, in order to help middle-income students, who were likely to receive less money from the federal government.

What can be said about the status of student financial aid today? The passage of MISAA should alleviate some of the financial burden facing middle-income families, thus freeing up some institutional funds that were previously used to augment federal aid programs based on need. The impact of MISAA in freeing up institutional funds, however, has been lessened by recent legislation in which the maximum amount of Pell Grants to every recipient was reduced by $130. Furthermore, if inflation continues to run at the current annual rate of 12 percent, the cost of attending a college or university will go up, and the financial resources of middle-income families may be reduced to the extent that expected family contribution, or what a family is willing to pay for a child's college education, is also significantly reduced. In this case, the benefit of MISAA would be reduced and the pressure on institutions, especially private institutions, to use their own funds to meet the financial need of middle-income students would be increased. (At this writing, the benefits resulting from MISAA will likely be negated because Congress, now in the process of reconciling the 1982 federal budget, seems to be accepting most of President Reagan's budget recommendations.)

Institutionally funded student aid has a substantial role in providing equal educational opportunity to students. Although the federal government has assumed the primary role in providing equal opportunity, institutions fulfill several functions in providing aid to students: (1) promoting access and choice, particularly at high-tuition institutions; (2) maintaining aid until degree completion; (3) supplementing federal and state aid for students of all income levels; and (4) assisting middle-income students and other students who are not always eligible for aid under public programs.

III

Institutionally Funded Student Aid and Selective Recruitment of Students

Options in Targeting Institutional Aid

Colleges and universities have considerable latitude in selecting recipients of institutionally funded student aid and in determining the size of awards. Most institutionally funded student aid (approximately 84 percent) comes from unrestricted general institutional funds and is allocated in the form of need-based awards, academic merit awards, athletic awards, tuition remissions, and employment funds (see table 3.1). Aid from restricted gifts and endowments is limited to students who fulfill certain requirements, such as those pertaining to state

TABLE 3.1

PERCENT DISTRIBUTION OF THE FORMS OF INSTITUTIONALLY FUNDED UNDERGRADUATE STUDENT AID, BY SOURCE OF AID, 1976-77

Forms of Aid	Total Institutional Aid	Restricted Endowment Income	Restricted Gifts	Unrestricted General Funds
Total dollars (in thousands)	$1,407,100	$104,800	$126,400	$1,175,900
Total percentage	100.0%	100.0%	100.0%	100.0%
Need-based awards	33.9	75.9	43.2	29.2
Academic merit awards	9.0	16.2	19.2	7.2
Athletic awards	7.6	3.7	24.0	6.2
Tuition remissions	7.3	0.9	0.7	8.6
Employment funds	39.1	1.6	6.2	45.9
Other	3.1	1.7	6.7	2.8

SOURCE: Irene L. Gomberg and Frank J. Atelsek, "The Institutional Share of Undergraduate Financial Assistance, 1976-77," Higher Education Panel Report no. 42 (Washington, D.C.: American Council on Education, May 1979), p. 18.

residence and grade point averages, for example. Such aid is part of the institution's complete aid program and in many cases replaces funds that would have been drawn from unrestricted sources.

Institutionally funded student aid may be divided into two categories: (1) need-based awards and (2) merit-based awards. Institutional policy makers must decide how much institutional aid is to be distributed primarily on the basis of student financial need and how much on the basis of other criteria. Need-based institutional aid is generally used to augment federal and state need-based programs, thus promoting greater access to college for prospective students who would otherwise have difficulty paying for their education.

Alternatively, institutional funds may be awarded to students who have special academic abilities or other skills that the institution feels would help round out the student body or increase its prestige. In this case, institutional aid is based on merit and is used to recruit those students that an institution wishes to enroll.

The previous chapter discussed need-based awards; this chapter will review merit-based awards. A college may wish to attract students with exceptional academic ability or students who are athletically or artistically gifted. In other instances, a college may wish to recruit students who have had leadership experience, including involvement in community and religious activities. In addition, an institution may use institutional aid to attract students from different regions or from foreign countries in order to make the student body more diverse. Institutions are not ignorant of the multiple purposes of grant aid; for example, many aid programs base their awards on academic merit but base the *amount* of the award on financial need.

Benefits of Targeting Institutional Aid for Students with Special Abilities

The use of institutional aid for selective recruitment can greatly benefit a college or university. An institution's reputation may be enhanced through an influx of bright and gifted students. Students may be better matched to programmatic offerings, more receptive to the academic program, and less likely to drop out.

In addition, an institution may benefit from students' talents and abilities as they enrich the academic and cultural life on campus. When institutional aid is used to recruit student athletes, additional benefits may acrue to the institution. A successful athletic program

32 Selective Recruitment of Students

TABLE 3.2

PEAKS AND TROUGHS IN SIZE OF PARTICULAR AGE GROUPS, 1978–2000 (size in millions)

Age Group	Peak Year	Peak Size	Trough Year	Trough Size	Decline from Peak to Trough
18-year-olds	1979	4.29	1992	3.17	25%
18–21-year-olds	1979	17.16	1994	12.97	24%
18–24-year-olds	1981	29.51	1996	22.86	23%

SOURCE: Kenneth M. Deitch, "Pricing and Financial Aid in American Higher Education: Some Interactions," Sloan Commission on Government and Higher Education, preliminary draft, 14 August 1978, p. 2.

can be an extremely valuable asset that attracts revenue from alumni and other sources. Selective targeting of institutional aid can therefore determine or change the mix of students in ways that may improve an institution's reputation and its financial health.

Institutional Aid and Competition for Students

Competition between colleges and universities for bright and talented students encourages institutions to use their institutionally funded student aid for the selective recruitment of students. Because the pool of academically, artistically, and athletically talented students is limited, institutions compete for the same applicants not only with their peers but with institutions of all types—four-year, two-year, public, and private.

McPherson's seminal paper on the competition between public and private institutions concludes that both types of institutions often appeal to similar clienteles. State colleges and the less selective private institutions are cases in point: both compete for students who are quite similar in terms of income, career ambitions, ability, and family background.[1]

Furthermore, the competition for high school graduates may intensify in the future. Demographic projections indicate that the number of 18–24-year-olds in America will markedly decline in the 1990s (see table 3.2). This shrinking population base strongly suggests, but does not guarantee, that aggregate enrollment in postsecondary education will decline. Conceivably, increased participation by women, minority students, and older persons may offset the decline in

1. Michael S. McPherson, "The Demand for Higher Education," in *Public Policy and Private Higher Education*, eds. David W. Breneman and Chester E. Finn, Jr. (Washington, D.C.: The Brookings Institution, 1978), p. 194.

TABLE 3.3

PERCENT AND DOLLAR DISTRIBUTION OF FORMS OF INSTITUTIONALLY FUNDED UNDERGRADUATE STUDENT AID, 1976-77, BY INSTITUTIONAL CONTROL

Forms of Aid	Public Institutions Dollars (in thousands)	%	Private Institutions Dollars (in thousands)	%
Academic merit grants	$ 59,240	8.6	$ 67,520	9.4
Athletics grants	61,990	9.0	45,250	6.3
Tuition remissions	22,700	3.3	80,400	11.2
Need-based grants	118,500	17.2	359,200	50.0
Employment funds	398,100	57.8	150,800	21.0

SOURCE: Based on Irene L. Gomberg and Frank J. Atelsek, "The Institutional Share of Undergraduate Financial Assistance, 1976-77," Higher Education Panel Report no. 42 (Washington, D.C.: American Council on Education, May 1979), p. 18.

the number of 18–24-year-olds, the traditional college-age population.

Increasing rates of enrollment within these groups may not, however, fully compensate for the decline of the traditional college-age population.[2] Thus, colleges and universities—especially private institutions, whose tuition is already very high—can anticipate some difficult recruiting years. Competition for students may intensify, and some institutions may experience difficulty in filling classrooms. Institutions unable to attract an adequate number of students will strive to stabilize enrollment by increasing their allocations of institutionally funded aid for the purpose of recruitment.

Of course, increases in the outflow of institutionally funded student aid will, to some extent, negate the financial benefit of greater numbers of students. Many colleges may find themselves caught in a vicious cycle in which the need for more tuition-paying students increases the need for institutional student aid to attract these students. This cycle, which results in a loss of funds for other important institutional programs, can also have a negative effect on an institution's quality, reputation, and financial vitality.

Institutional Aid and Recruitment of Students

Competition for highly qualified students has prompted many colleges and universities to use their institutional aid to recruit students

2. Kenneth M. Deitch, "Pricing and Financial Aid in American Higher Education: Some Interactions," Sloan Commission on Government and Higher Education, preliminary draft, 14 August 1975, p. 2.

on the basis of ability and talent. Public and private institutions target similar amounts and proportions of their institutionally funded student aid for awards to academically and athletically gifted students.

Data generated by the American Council on Education–Higher Education Panel survey indicate that in 1976–77 private institutions disbursed $67.5 million (9.4 percent) of their institutional aid to recruit students on the basis of academic merit; in addition they awarded $45 million (6.3 percent) to student athletes (see table 3.3). Public institutions allocated similar amounts of their institutional aid to desired students. They used $59 million (8.6 percent) of their institutional aid to attract students with academic ability; $62 million (9 percent) went to student athletes. Public institutions distribute these funds to many more students than do private institutions; thus the size of the average grant awarded by public institutions is considerably smaller than the size of the average grant awarded by private institutions.

Table 3.4 shows the range of institutional policies regarding the

TABLE 3.4

INSTITUTIONS THAT PROVIDED FINANCIAL INDUCEMENTS FOR ACCEPTED APPLICANTS TO ENROLL

		All Institutions	Two-year Public	Two-year Private	Four-year Public	Four-year Private
No-need scholarships used	No.	751	124	35	199	393
	%	51%	31%	43%	60%	61%
Modifications in packaging used	No.	496	83	20	91	302
	%	34%	21%	25%	27%	47%
No-need scholarships or modifications in packaging offered to applicants from the following groups:						
Athletes	No.	654	126	25	211	292
	%	45%	31%	31%	63%	45%
Racial or ethnic minorities	No.	381	71	12	108	190
	%	26%	18%	15%	32%	29%
Disadvantaged students	No.	318	72	12	77	157
	%	22%	18%	15%	23%	24%
Students with special non-academic talents	No.	579	112	28	176	263
	%	40%	28%	35%	53%	41%
Academically talented students	No.	890	145	44	241	460
	%	61%	36%	54%	72%	71%
Students from different geographic locations	No.	174	35	7	44	88
	%	12%	9%	9%	13%	14%
Total number of institutions		1,463	401	81	333	648

SOURCE: Reprinted with permission from *Undergraduate Admissions: The Realities of Institutional Policies, Practices, and Procedures*, copyright 1980 by College Entrance Examination Board, New York, p. 42.

TABLE 3.5

DISTRIBUTION OF INSTITUTIONALLY FUNDED UNDERGRADUATE
GRANTS AND TUITION REMISSIONS, 1978-79,
BY INSTITUTIONAL TYPE AND CONTROL

	Tuition		Need-based Grants	Ability-based Grants	Tuition Remissions	Total Awards*
Private Institutions						
Four year, high tuition	>$2,500	No. %	120,017 65%	47,478 26%	16,919 9%	100%
Four year, low tuition	<$2,500	No. %	19,204 18%	51,437 47%	38,609 35%	100%
Two year, high tuition*	>$1,200	No. %	10,709 49%	9,802 45%	1,185 6%	100%
Public Institutions						
Four year, high tuition	>$700	No. %	69,049 44%	67,092 43%	19,325 13%	100%
Four year, low tuition	<$700	No. %	40,701 48%	19,918 24%	24,066 28%	100%
Two year, high tuition	>$300	No. %	3,449 5%	12,167 17%	55,971 78%	100%

*Duplicated counts included to make totals.
**Two-year, low-tuition institutions have been excluded because of the low numbers of awards.
SOURCE: Based on Patricia A. Smith, Paula R. Knepper, Janet P. Jackley, and Cathy Henderson, "Financing Undergraduate Education in 1978-79," Policy Analysis Service (Washington, D.C.: American Council on Education, June 1980), pp. 21-27.

use of no-need scholarships. A majority of all institutions and 60 percent of four-year institutions, both public and private, provided these inducements, while only 31 percent of public two-year institutions did. Nearly three-fourths of all four-year institutions provided some merit scholarships for academically talented students. Most four-year institutions also recruited student athletes; 63 percent of all public four-year and 45 percent of all private four-year institutions did so. Less common, however, were no-need scholarships for racial or ethnic minority students, disadvantaged students, and students from different geographic locations.

Selective Targeting of Institutional Aid by Institutional Type and Control

When the number of grants rather than the total funds awarded is analyzed by type and control of institution, institutions show less similarity in their patterns of awarding aid. Data collected from the AMS study of campus-based grant programs and analyzed by the

American Council on Education indicate that the number of students aided with institutional funds varies markedly by institutional type and control.

According to table 3.5, in 1978–79 private four-year, low-tuition institutions and public two-year, high-tuition institutions allocated more institutionally funded grants on the basis of academic ability than on the basis of need. In contrast, private four-year, high-tuition institutions and public four-year, low-tuition institutions allocated more institutionally funded grants on the basis of need than on the basis of ability. Public four-year, high-tuition institutions and private two-year, high-tuition institutions fell somewhere in between: they tended to award their institutionally funded grants equally on the basis of need and ability.

The data suggest that private four-year, low-tuition institutions and public two-year, high-tuition institutions place the greatest priority on using institutionally funded grants to recruit selectively students on the basis of their abilities and skills. These instituitons may have the greatest difficulty in attracting highly qualified students and must, therefore, adopt aid policies that make them more competitive. In addition, the tuition costs of these institutions may be low enough to reduce the necessity for need-based grants, thus freeing funds for ability-based awards.

On the other hand, private four-year, high-tuition institutions and public four-year, low-tuition institutions may more easily attract bright students and thus feel less pressure to target their institutionally funded grant aid for merit-based awards. The private high-tuition institutions must make many need-based awards because of their high tuition. The public low-tuition institutions may not have a high priority for attracting students showing great ability because of their open availability to all qualified students. Both types of institutions thus favor need-based awards.

Need-based grants awarded by more selective private colleges and universities may actually serve two purposes: (1) to make it possible for students of all income levels to attend the institution and (2) to attract academically talented students. Because of the stringent admissions standards of these selective institutions, a need-based institutionally funded grant may also be regarded as a reward for academic achievement.

Indeed, 1976 data gathered by the Cooperative Institutional Research Program (CIRP), the Higher Education Research Labo-

TABLE 3.6

REASONS CITED BY STUDENTS FOR RECEIVING AID, AS PERCENTAGE OF STUDENTS RECEIVING INSTITUTIONAL AID

Basis for Aid	Not a Reason		Minor Reason		Major Reason	
Financial need	13.4%	(14.0%)*	13.9%	(13.8%)	72.7%	(72.2%)
Academic talent	20.4	(46.9)	33.0	(32.8)	46.6	(20.3)
Athletic talent	87.3	(86.2)	6.7	(7.0)	5.9	(6.8)

*Figures in parentheses represent percentage of students who receive any form of aid. Aid may be received from multiple sources.

SOURCE: Unpublished 1978 analysis of 1976 Cooperative Institutional Research Program data, Policy Analysis Service, American Council on Education.

ratory at UCLA, and the American Council on Education suggest the existence of dual-purpose aid. In the CIRP questionnaire, students were asked their perceptions about the reasons they received aid. The questionnaire was designed to accommodate replies acknowledging multiple sources and multiple purposes. The results show that 80 percent of the students receiving institutionally funded grants (and, perhaps, other grants) saw their grant as a reward for academic talent (see table 3.6). In addition, nearly 87 percent saw need as a basis for their award. Hence, many students perceived both need and academic ability as the basis for their award.

Forty-seven percent of students receiving institutional aid cited academic talents as a major reason for receiving aid, whereas only 20

TABLE 3.7

PERCENT DISTRIBUTION OF TYPE OF INSTITUTIONALLY FUNDED AID TO FRESHMEN, BY HIGH SCHOOL GRADE AVERAGES, 1976-77

High School Grades	Institutional Grant Only	Institutional Loan Only	Institutional Loan and Grant	National Norm for All Sources
A or A+	23.4%	7.6%	17.5%	8.6%
A−	20.9	11.0	17.3	11.1
B+	22.9	22.4	21.6	20.3
B	18.2	27.4	21.7	27.6
B−	6.9	12.1	9.0	13.6
C+	4.8	12.4	7.6	11.4
C	2.6	6.6	4.7	7.0
D	0.2	0.4	0.5	0.4
Total	100.0	100.0	100.0	100.0

SOURCE: Unpublished 1978 analysis of 1976 Cooperative Institutional Research Program data, Policy Analysis Service, American Council on Education.

percent of students receiving any kind of aid cited academic talents as a reason for receiving aid. These data support the premise that academically talented students are more likely to receive institutional aid than federal or state aid.

The dual purpose of institutional data is also revealed by CIRP data concerning the relationship between awards granted and high school grade point averages. Forty-four percent of students receiving institutionally funded grants had high school grade averages of A or A−, despite the fact that these students represented only 20 percent of the national freshman class receiving aid (see table 3.7).

These data suggest that, in many instances, institutionally funded grants are given to students who show both academic talent and financial need. Moreover, dual-purpose aid is more likely to occur in selective private colleges and universities that attract many bright and talented applicants.

Both public and private postsecondary institutions are using about one-sixth of their institutionally funded student aid to recruit selectively students with outstanding academic or athletic credentials (see table 3.1). Whether institutions will continue to give priority to the awarding of institutional aid to talented students is difficult to ascertain. On one hand, the intangible reward of having these students present on campus will certainly not decline, and the difficulty of attracting students of the traditional college age will increase. Competition for the most talented students may escalate as the competition for all students escalates. Institutions will, as a result, be under more pressure to use institutionally funded student aid for the selective recruitment of talented students.

On the other hand, the increasing difficulty of ensuring that revenue grows as quickly as expenditures will force institutions to consider reducing the number and size of merit-based awards. Aid will be targeted only for students with financial need, while awards to the talented will become increasingly less financial (honors programs, for example). State and federal student aid programs allow institutions to stretch their aid funds, and the institutions themselves can use institutional aid to attract talented students who qualify for federal and state aid. This synergy exists only for needy students: federal and state aid is not designed to attract talented students with no financial need.

A growing concern among institutions is the prevention of wastefulness that occurs when merit-based institutional aid is awarded to students who would have attended the institution in any case. As the data presented in this chapter show, the awarding of dual-purpose institutional aid—i.e., aid awarded on the basis of both financial need and academic achievement—is an important tool in preventing waste and building the kind of student body that the institution wishes to enroll.

IV
Institutionally Funded Student Aid and Institutional Vitality

Institutionally funded student aid is one factor that affects an institution's financial health. Student aid drawn from an institution's own funds plays a role in pricing education, which in turn influences the demand for and perceived value of the educational experience. Institutional aid also affects institutional enrollment and, hence, the inflow of revenue.

The interaction between institutionally funded student aid, price, and demand is complex. An institution's gross price is equivalent to tuition and required fees.[1] Many families, however, do not have to absorb the entire cost of a student's education. Through federal, state, and institutional financial aid programs, the price is significantly reduced for a majority of college and university students. The result is *net price*, which will be defined as tuition and required fees minus grant assistance. Because the amount of grant assistance varies greatly from student to student, each institution may charge many net prices.

Institutional Aid, Net Price, and Maximizing Revenue

From the standpoint of optimum financial health (thus neglecting for a moment the issues discussed in previous chapters relating to student opportunity, student body characteristics, and social equity), an institution's pricing policy should be related to its market in such a way as to maximize revenue. Theoretically, revenue from tuition can be maximized by adjusting the net price upward or downward to influence enrollment and improve the institution's market position.

---

1. *Gross price*, as used here, does not include room and board or income foregone by attending a postsecondary institution.

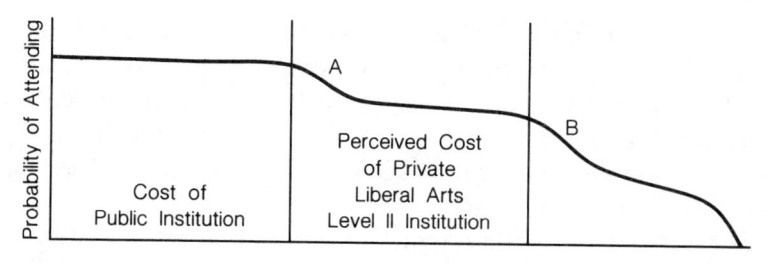

Fig. 4.1. Hypothetical relationship between cost of a private liberal arts level II institution and the probability of attending the institution

The net price can be adjusted by increasing or decreasing the amount of price discounting—e.g., by offering greater or lesser grant assistance—and by changing the level of tuition and fees. In practice, of course, maximizing revenue requires complex and tricky manipulation.

The relationship between enrollment, tuition, revenue, and aid is a relatively simple one. Enrollment is determined when prospective students decide to attend an institution. Tuition cost is a factor in this decision. A hypothetical relationship between the probability of the prospective student's attending the institution and the perceived cost for each potential student is shown in figure 4.1. The hypothesis is that within certain ranges, changes in perceived cost affect only slightly the decision to attend an institution. As long as the cost is "reasonable," other factors are more important. If a private, liberal arts, Level II college is taken as an example, the curve is discontinuous at the point at which tuition for public institutions is perceived to lie and at the point at which tuition for selective colleges is perceived to lie (see points A and B in figure 4.1). As a result, a liberal arts college that awards a bachelor's degree and whose tuition is below that of public institutions would probably experience high enrollment.

Perceived price, which differs for each person, is a complex notion that takes into account gross price, known scholarships, and estimates of overall hardship. Gross price is an important determinant of perceived price, especially when announcements about awards of aid are delayed by uncertainties in the regulations. Known scholarships include entitlements of which the entering student is aware. Institutional awards made to applicants at the time that they are accepted by the institution may also change their perception of institutional price, especially if they have a choice of institutions.

Students who must deplete savings, work during the summer or the school year, borrow money, or consume family income to attend an institution will include a hardship factor in their perceived price calculations. Not all students are willing to borrow money or to work. A job on campus lowers the perceived price, but not as much as would a scholarship of equal amount.

The institution partially controls the net price of tuition. To determine the total net tuition revenue, the institution can multiply the price by the enrollment and then deduct the amount of institutional aid.

An estimate of potential enrollment can be derived by estimating the probability of each potential student's attending the institution. Perceived price is roughly related to net price. Figure 4.2 provides a hypothesis for this relationship.

In this figure, enrollment declines as net price increases. At points A and B, the transition to lower enrollment because of higher net price is more gradual because the graph is a summation of each person's probability of attending the institution. Each student perceives the tuition level of public and private institutions differently. The summation thus causes the transition from higher to lower enrollment to occur gradually.

The enrollment curve in figure 4.2 is not as steep as the curve in figure 4.1 because net price is only one factor that determines perceived price. The relationship between enrollment and net price is important because it directly affects tuition revenue. When net price is zero, revenue is zero. When enrollment is zero, revenue is, again, zero. At some point in between, a maximum level of revenue is reached. Two important formulae summarizing this relationship follow:

Net revenue per student = Tuition rate − Unrestricted institutionally funded student aid ÷ Total FTE

Revenue = Net revenue per student × Enrollment

Also note that the bell-shaped revenue curve in figure 4.2 would be much flatter if the enrollment response curve were flatter.

To develop an array of net prices in order to maximize revenue in the short term (one year) but especially for the longer term (for example, five years), an institution must undertake several complex investigations. First, the institution must identify its potential market. It must also evaluate the market's potential according to demographic

```
Enrollment  ┌─────
            │         ╱‾‾‾╲   Maximum Revenue
            │      ╱        ╲
            │   ╱     ‾‾‾‾‾‾‾╲___
Revenue     └╱_____╲___
                Net Price
       (tuition less institutional financial aid
              from unrestricted funds)
```

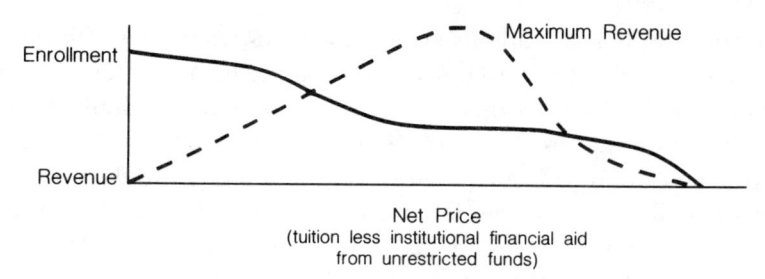

Fig. 4.2. Hypothetical relationship between revenue, enrollment, and net price of private liberal arts level II institution

projections and the projected value of academic degrees. Next, various kinds of research, including price elasticity research, must be conducted to determine how revenue can be maximized in relation to the potential market. Ihlanfeldt underscores the focus of such research:

> To achieve this end, an institution must study the probable effects of a change in price in relation to both the changes in availability of government financial assistance and the changes in per capita disposable income among the institution's primary market. The focus of such a study should be the net tuition students are paying on a per capita basis and the extent to which tuition increases have paralleled increases in per capita disposable income or after-tax income over a given period of time.[2]

Conducting such a study is a difficult task. An institution can make a preliminary assessment of the effectiveness of current pricing policies by computing trends in the mean family income of the students.[3] Next, it can compute trends in the dispersion of student family income. (Standard deviation is probably the best measure.) The institution can then plot these trends with the mean family income. The resulting figure can provide some guidance for formulating pricing policy and allocating institutionally funded student aid.

Trends in mean family income help determine the appropriate direction of trends in tuition, while trends in the dispersion of family income help determine the need for changes in tuition discounting policy through allocations of institutionally funded aid. For example,

---

2. William Ihlanfeldt, *Achieving Optimal Enrollments and Tuition Revenues* (San Francisco: Jossey-Bass, 1980), p. 103.

3. It is assumed that an institution has enrolled its student body on the basis of a well-articulated and continuing mission. If, however, a college or university is planning to change the composition of its student body, it will have to project changes in the family income of the students caused by changes in admission policies.

an institution whose students are homogenous with respect to family income—i. e., the standard deviation of family income is low—should be able to keep gross tuition in line with trends in mean family income and keep expenditures of institutionally funded aid low in order to maximize tuition revenue. Thus, for instance, institutions whose students reflect a low mean family income and a small standard deviation in family income (as is the case with many Southern, traditionally black colleges and school A in figure 4.3) should adopt a pricing policy in which a low gross tuition is matched with a reduction or elimination of institutionally funded student aid that discounts tuition for some students.

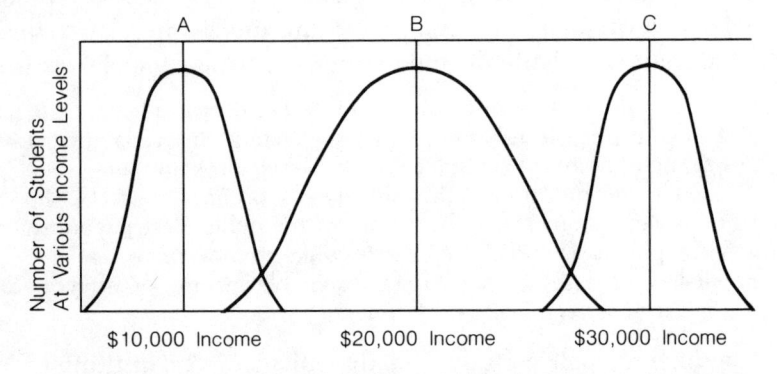

A—Low mean family income ($10,000); small standard deviation. Low tuition; small outlay of institutionally funded student financial aid required.

B—Middle mean family income ($20,000); large standard deviation. Moderate tuition; large outlay of institutionally funded student financial aid required.

C—High mean family income ($30,000); small standard deviation. High tuition; small outlay of institutionally funded student financial aid required.

Fig. 4.3. Student market study—plot of mean family income versus standard deviation of student family income for three possible situations

Institutions with students from lower-income families will find raising tuition difficult because they have so few students who can afford higher tuition. To secure more income, such institutions might ask its few students from middle-income families to pay more, and the students from lower-income families might be given greater institutional aid subsidies to make up the difference.

Yet many institutions still feel that the risks of this approach outweigh the benefits. The benefits include (1) more revenue from the few students who can afford the higher tuition and (2) the possibility of increased aid from government programs based on increased computed need. The risks include losing applicants from low-income families who comprehend only the high gross tuition price when deciding whether to attend the institution. These students may decide to go elsewhere, especially if competing institutions do not also raise their costs, and enrollment problems will only be compounded. Finally, although students from middle-income families may comprise only 10 percent of an institution's enrollment, the loss of students from lower-income families because of higher tuition could severely damage the collegial atmosphere and faculty morale. These students may be among the institution's most promising and may be models for other students from less affluent backgrounds. Hence, most institutions are reluctant to raise tuition.

Institutions whose students reflect a high mean family income and a narrow standard deviation from this mean (for example, some highly selective institutions, like school C in figure 4.3) should adopt a policy of high tuition with a small expenditure of institutionally funded student aid. Students are less likely to enroll at these institutions if they do not receive some discount on tuition.

On the other hand, institutions with students representing a broad spectrum of family incomes (as at many private, urban institutions and as in school B in figure 4.3) should set gross tuition in line with mean family income and plan to allocate greater amounts of institutionally funded student aid for price discounting. The greater the range of family income, the more institutionally funded student aid is needed to make the net price of the institution affordable to all students in the market. If the institution's analysis shows that its student body is becoming more economically diverse, then increases in the institutional aid allocation are needed.

Evaluation of students' family income is, of course, only a preliminary assessment of one factor of institutional pricing policy. Other variables that must be considered include the per capita disposable income for an institution's primary market, changes in the availability of government financial assistance, and the pricing policy of similar, nearby institutions.

Many institutions by-pass the research that Ihlanfeldt proposes by identifying the tuition costs of similar institutions and placing themselves "appropriately" in that range. Although the assessment of competitive costs is an important step in developing a tuition strategy, it does not provide much information about the amount of institutionally funded student aid that should be allocated.

Market Position and Pricing Models

An institution's market position is determined by its reputation, programs, location, and tuition costs. To a certain extent, tuition itself also affects reputation. To make the most effective use of market position, the institution must manipulate these factors in such a way that it faces the fewest competitors for the most students willing to pay the highest tuition. Few institutions are likely to be able to change the first three factors significantly in the short run, so pricing policy becomes critical.

In attempting to maximize their market positions and revenue, colleges and universities may wish to explore different pricing models before developing policies for the use of financial assistance.[4] Traditionally, the common tuition model has been equity, or variable, pricing, in which the same gross price is charged to all students. Other variable pricing patterns, however, may better suit the distinctive character and mission of a particular institution.

Some important institutional characteristics to be considered in setting pricing policy are the proportion of part-time students (often a result of an institution's mission to serve a community), the potential of unused dormitories, and the potential of unused classrooms. An institution's mission influences these characteristics by setting priorities for the types of students it wishes to recruit and admit—their academic preparedness, geographic distribution, financial status, and inherent retention characteristics.

The two basic forms of variable pricing are differential pricing and graduated pricing. Under a differential pricing policy, an institution charges prices that vary according to the student's circumstances. For instance, institutions with full dormitories and full classroom space are now experimenting with a differentiated tuition for students who graduate from local high schools and who choose to live at home. In this way, institutions can aid local students in saving money, increase enrollment, reduce the pressure on dormitories, and use academic space and time more efficiently.

Under a graduated pricing policy, an institution charges a student a set rate based on his or her year in school. Freshmen pay less than

4. For a more detailed description of pricing models, see Ihlanfeldt, Chapter 6, "Pricing Educational Programs."

seniors, and seniors pay less than graduate students. According to Ihlanfeldt, this form of pricing is more closely related to the cost of providing the educational service than is differential pricing.[5]

Furthermore, variable pricing patterns can be applied to four basic pricing models: (1) scaled pricing; (2) two-part pricing; (3) term pricing; and (4) unit pricing. In scaled pricing, the student is charged a fee for both the first and second courses, a lower fee for additional courses up to the accepted norm (for example, sixteen credit hours), and a higher fee for additional courses above the accepted norm. Two-part pricing divides tuition into two parts: a fixed price associated with the process of enrolling and a price per course. Term pricing entails a flat tuition that is charged each term; a student may take as few or as many courses as desired. Unit pricing charges students a set amount per course.

Ihlanfeldt notes that each pricing model is suited to a particular kind of postsecondary institution depending on institutional type and control as well as institutional mission and market. For example, unit pricing is most useful in attracting part-time students from the nearby area; thus it is a viable policy option for colleges attempting to bring in more local students.[6]

To the extent that a student is not paying the exact, full price of his or her unit cost of education, a subsidy is being provided. The pricing structures discussed above offer direct "discounts" or "marginal" prices. Institutionally funded student aid offers a discount in the form of a "rebate" lure instead.

Institutionally Funded Student Aid, Net Price, and Market Position

The strength of an institution's market position is determined by the complex interaction of the institution's pricing policy, its offers of financial aid, the quality and variety of its educational offerings, its accessibility and geographical location, its reputation, and the composition of the student body. All these variables have an effect on student demand for education at that particular college or university.

Highly prestigious independent institutions with strong national market positions generally have little difficulty in filling their classrooms with qualified students. Should rising operating costs demand

---

5. Ihlanfeldt, p. 116.
6. *Ibid.*, pp. 115–23.

that revenue from tuition increase, these institutions are in a position to adjust their net prices upward with little fear of adverse results. These elite private colleges and universities, however, make up only a small fraction of all postsecondary institutions. According to Ihlanfeldt, the number of these independent institutions does not exceed seventy-five.[7]

On the other hand, most colleges and universities have weaker markets, and for these institutions net price plays a greater role in attracting students. A review of several demand studies indicates that, in many instances, price affects enrollment. That is, if net price is increased, enrollment will drop; if net price is decreased, enrollment will rise. There is much disagreement about the effect of price, especially given the changing and discontinuous relationship between price and enrollment. The most quoted finding, however, is that a $100 cut in tuition occurring in all institutions simultaneously would lead to about a 1 percent increase in the enrollment rate (expressed as a percentage of 18–24-year-olds).[8]

TABLE 4.1

REASONS GIVEN BY FRESHMEN FOR ATTENDING A PARTICULAR INSTITUTION, BY LEVEL OF IMPORTANCE

Reason	Freshmen Receiving College Aid			All Freshmen
	Not Important	Somewhat Important	Important	Very Important
Academic reputation of institution	6.6%	36.1%	57.2%	43.1%
Offer of financial assistance	23.6	34.6	41.8	13.6
Low tuition of institution	63.8	25.5	10.8	18.0
Recruitment by college representative	75.1	17.3	7.7	3.9

SOURCE: Unpublished 1978 analysis of 1976 Cooperative Institutional Research Program data, Policy Analysis Service, American Council on Education.

The importance of institutionally funded student aid in influencing the decision to attend a particular institution can be seen in table 4.1. These data, from the CIRP survey, reflect the degree to which an offer of institutional aid affects a potential student's decision to attend an institution. Evidently, institutional aid was a major factor in the student's decision to attend a particular institution. Forty-two percent of the freshmen receiving institutional aid said that financial assis-

7. Ibid., p. 97.

8. See Michael S. McPherson, "The Demand for Higher Education," in *Public Policy and Higher Education*, eds. David W. Breneman and Chester E. Finn, Jr. (Washington, D.C.: The Brookings Institution, 1978).

tance was a very important reason for attending the institution; only 13.6 percent of *all* freshmen rated financial assistance as very important.

Other variables also strongly interact with the effect of price, and these variables include family income and institutional type and control. For example, many studies find that youth from low-income families are more responsive to price changes than are youth from upper-income families. In a 1975 study, Carlson estimated that a $100 cut in tuition would increase by 8 percent the enrollment rate of youth from families with an income ranging from zero to $6,000. On the other hand, the enrollment rate of youth from families with an income over $9,000 per year would increase by only about 1.5 percent.[9] In addition, many studies find that prospective students are more responsive to price changes at certain types of institutions.[10] The complex relationship between price and these other variables underscores the need for institutions to assess their students' responsiveness to price and to heed these findings when setting policy for tuition and financial aid.

Theoretically, marginal differences in the market positions of institutions could be neutralized through increased offers of institutionally funded aid. In practice, however, this approach may not work. For institutions with weak market positions, increased allocations of institutionally funded aid can put them in a weaker financial state. That is, a college unable to attract a desired number of students can attempt to upgrade its enrollment by increasing offers of institutionally funded student aid, thereby adjusting net price downward. If, however, marginal operating costs (which include increased student aid costs, increased energy costs, and increased consumption of academic supplies) exceed marginal revenue for each new student partly subsidized by institutionally funded aid, the college's financial condition will be made worse. A policy to aid new students with institutional funds may therefore threaten the college's financial health. The danger is even greater if the policy of additional aid is extended to *all* students, not just those most responsive to net price changes, as must often be the case.

9. See Daryl Carlson, "A Flow of Funds Model for Assessing the Impact of Alternative Student Aid Programs" (Washington, D.C.: Department of Health, Education, and Welfare, November 1975).

10. See Carlson. See also Roy Radner and Leonard S. Miller, *Demand and Supply in U.S. Higher Education*, Carnegie Commission on Higher Education (New York: McGraw-Hill, 1975).

Unfortunately, isolating the impact of institutionally funded aid on an institution's financial condition is difficult because so many factors are involved. A current study, by the American Council on Education, of institutional financial conditions reveals that from fiscal year 1975 to fiscal year 1978 many independent, four-year (nonuniversity) institutions achieved net surpluses in their current fund accounts while *increasing* the amount of aid per student awarded from unrestricted funds (see table 4.2).

TABLE 4.2

NUMBER OF FOUR-YEAR INDEPENDENT COLLEGES (NON-UNIVERSITY) MAKING CHANGES IN AMOUNT OF AID FROM UNRESTRICTED FUNDS, FY1975 to FY1978

	Less Aid Per Student From Unrestricted Funds	More Aid Per Student From Unrestricted Funds
Net surplus (current fund balance increase)	94	357
Net deficit (current fund balance decrease)	81	246

SOURCE: Finance survey data, National Center for Education Statistics.

An increase in institutional aid to students is thus not, by itself, a sign of institutional financial difficulty. Nevertheless, an institution's ability to attract students with financial aid from its own resources is, in fact, limited.

Ihlanfeldt introduces another option for improving an institution's market position. He suggests that institutional funds earmarked for student aid might be better utilized in improving the quality of instruction. Rather than attempting to improve the college's market position by price discounting, institutional policy makers might consider the alternative—upgrading the educational experience for undergraduates. Educational excellence generates satisfied students, who, in turn, become salespersons for the institution. According to Ihlanfeldt, this is the first step in improving an institution's market position.[11]

Institutionally Funded Student Aid, Institutional Vitality, and the Competition for Students

Institutional vitality depends not only on maximization of revenue but also on recruitment of desired students and, in times of adversity,

11. Ihlanfeldt, p. 110.

stabilization of enrollment. Vitality includes financial security and academic program strength. The competition among colleges and universities for bright and talented students, mentioned in the previous chapter, affects institutional vitality.

Competition for students occurs among a wide variety of public and private postsecondary institutions. In light of demographic projections indicating that the number of 18–24-year-old Americans will markedly decline by the 1990s, the competition for students will probably intensify in the future. For some institutions, the primary challenge arising from increased competition will not be maintaining a given enrollment of a given quality but simply surviving—by appealing to new student markets and maintaining minimum levels of enrollment.

Various strategies may be used to meet the critical squeeze caused by this competition. Institutions with strong market positions and similar reputations, comparable quality of offerings, and so forth can use institutionally funded grants to offset the advantage held by the lower-priced institutions. Similarly, institutions with weaker markets can elect to discount prices in response to the competition for students. At this point, Ihlanfeldt sounds a word of caution:

> ... a more satisfactory pricing policy may be one that balances the budget by reducing the gross tuition for all students while limiting or eliminating institutional financial aid that discounts the tuition for some students. For some independent schools, a lower tuition might broaden the potential market; for others, a higher tuition may be required to achieve the same objective.[12]

Whatever the case, the objective is to find the optimum balance between, on the one hand, an inflow of revenue from tuition and other sources and, on the other hand, a minimum acceptable level of enrollment. Logic dictates that public and private institutions with the strongest market positions are better equipped to strike this balance and consequently will best be able to weather the storm with respect to the competition for a dwindling pool of prospective students.

Institutionally Funded Student Aid and Competition between Public and Private Institutions

Recently, much attention has been focused on a related issue—the competition between public and private institutions for students. Several factors that relate to both external pressures and internal

---

12. *Ibid.*, p. 103.

institutional policies will influence the competition between public and private institutions as the period of enrollment decline approaches.[13]

External factors, which are largely beyond the control of the institution, include the projected decline in enrollment, the change in the perceived economic returns from a college degree, and the potential increase in enrollment among nontraditional clientele (older, part-time, and non-degree-credit students). Internal institutional factors include tuition pricing policies and other factors not related to price—admissions selectivity, quality and variety of offerings, institutional reputation, location, and so forth.[14] Foremost among these internal factors are institutional pricing policies and the resulting "tuition gap" between public and private institutions, in which public institutions operate at a significant price advantage over private institutions.

Despite methodological variations in recent studies focusing on the tuition gap, net tuition differences between public and private institutions appear to be increasing.[15] Although some types of independent institutions appear to have done better than others, many educators are concerned that, unless net price differences between public and independent institutions are reduced, private institutions will be priced out of the market. Some states—Ohio, for example—have helped keep private institutions viable by increasing tuition for public institutions and increasing government aid for students at private institutions.

When attempting to balance the price competition between public and private institutions, policy makers can consider a number of other options. Various demand studies suggest that when the net tuition gap widens, enrollment at public institutions will increase at the expense of enrollment at private institutions and that, in addition, a tuition cut at public institutions will attract a fair number of high-income students from private instititions.[16] McPherson comments:

13. For a more in-depth discussion of the competition between private and public institutions, see McPherson, pp. 145–96.

14. McPherson, p. 150.

15. See McPherson, pp. 167–68. See also Ihlanfeldt, p. 107.

16. See Gary T. Barnes, "Determinants of the College Going and College Choice Decision," processed (Greensboro, N. C.: University of North Carolina at Greensboro, 1973). See also Meir G. Kohn, Charles F. Manski, and David S. Mundel, "An Empirical Investigation of Factors Which Influence College Going Behaviors," R1740-NSF (Santa Monica, Calif.: Rand Corporation, 1974).

The striking implication for public policy is that if states were simultaneously to raise public tuition rates for high-income students and expand subsidies for low-income students, they could boost both private and total college enrollment at one stroke. By the same token, of course, policies to subsidize tuition rates at private institutions across the board would serve in good part to move relatively affluent students from public to private colleges (and to reduce the tuition bill for students who would attend private colleges anyway), and would do little compared to alternative uses of the same funds.[17]

In lieu of definitive action on the part of public policy makers, financial aid officers at private institutions have been using institutionally funded aid to reduce the price differential between public and private institutions. Data generated by a recent American Council on Education–Higher Education Panel survey indicate that during the 1976–77 academic year, institutionally funded student aid awards at private institutions averaged $1,227, including grants and employment, whereas institutionally funded student aid awards at public colleges and universities were considerably smaller, averaging $412 (see table 4.3).

TABLE 4.3

AVERAGE AMOUNT OF INSTITUTIONALLY FUNDED UNDERGRADUATE STUDENT AID, BY CATEGORY OF INSTITUTION, 1976–77

Category of Institution	Average Award Per Institutionally Aided Undergraduate	
	Grants and Employment	Grants, Employment, and Loans
Total	$ 627	$ 694
Total public	412	454
Universities	750	810
Four-year colleges	398	441
Two-year colleges	141	166
Total private	1,227	1,366
Universities	1,676	1,943
Four-year colleges	1,107	1,206
Two-year colleges[a]	511	593

[a]Data from private two-year colleges should be used with caution and only in conjunction with their standard errors as shown in Appendix Table C-6 of HEP Report no. 42.

SOURCE: Irene L. Gomberg and Frank J. Atelsek, "The Institutional Share of Undergraduate Financial Assistance, 1976–77," Higher Education Panel Report no. 42 (Washington, D.C.: American Council on Education, May 1979), p. 25.

17. McPherson, p. 186.

These differences are even more significant in light of the fact that 50 percent of institutionally funded student aid awarded by private institutions is used for need-based grants, whereas 58 percent of institutionally funded student aid awarded by public institutions is used for student employment funds. The data clearly suggest that independent colleges and universities are using their institutionally funded student aid to close the tuition gap and to become more competitive with public institutions.

How long private institutions can continue to divert funds from their own general operating revenue to institutionally funded student aid in order to narrow the net tuition gap is not clear. Institutions with relatively weak market positions may find themselves caught in a vicious cycle in which a growing tuition gap forces them to expend greater and greater amounts of institutionally funded student aid in order to attract students who, as a whole, pay commensurately less for their education. Certainly, these institutions will reach a point of diminishing returns: the expenditure of institutionally funded student aid will eventually surpass the inflow of revenue from tuition and other sources. These institutions will then have to seek other ways to improve their market position, perhaps, for example, by attempting to upgrade the quality of their educational offerings. In addition, they may seek to attract students who are not accustomed to rigorous academic demands. In so doing, these institutions will have to provide carefully tailored programs that most effectively promote the progress of these students. Increased recruiting that leads only to decreased retention will do little to improve the institution's viability.

V

Institutionally Funded Student Work Programs and Tuition Remissions

According to Higher Education Panel projections based on a survey of 1976–77 fiscal year expenditures, unrestricted institutional student aid funds that year totaled $1,176 billion. Forty-six percent of these funds was expended for student work programs. A smaller amount—9 percent, or over $101 million—was expended for tuition remissions.[1] Thus, the majority of aid to students from unrestricted institutional funds also procured direct benefits to the institution in the form of tasks completed by student workers and increased benefits to employees.

Only public institutions, however, awarded a majority of their unrestricted aid through these two programs. As table 5.1 shows, public institutions awarded 58 percent of their unrestricted aid funds to student employment programs, whereas private institutions

TABLE 5.1

DISTRIBUTION OF INSTITUTIONALLY FUNDED STUDENT AID (IFSA): EMPLOYMENT PROGRAMS AND TUITION REMISSIONS

	Employment Programs		Tuition Remissions	
	Amount	% of IFSA	Amount	% of IFSA
Public institutions	$398,500,000	57.8%	$22,800,000	3.3%
Private institutions	151,100,000	21.0	80,400,000	11.2

SOURCE: Irene L. Gomberg and Frank J. Atelsek, "The Institutional Share of Undergraduate Financial Assistance, 1976–77," Higher Education Panel Report no. 42 (Washington, D.C.: American Council on Education, May 1979), p. 18.

1. Irene L. Gomberg and Frank L. Atelsek, "The Institutional Share of Undergraduate Financial Assistance, 1976–77," Higher Education Panel Report no. 42 (Washington, D.C.: American Council on Education, May 1979), p. 18.

awarded only 21 percent of their unrestricted aid funds to student employment programs.

As noted earlier, private institutions award more of their unrestricted institutional aid as need-based grants than as student employment. In contrast, public institutions award a sizable portion of their institutional resources to student employment programs.

Some institutional funds are used to match federal work-study allocations. Under this program, the federal government provides 80 percent of a student's pay and the institution provides 20 percent from its own resources. Data show that in 1977 $111 million in institutional matching funds were required to match federal work-study funds. The same data broken down by institutional control show that public colleges spent 19 percent of their student employment funds to match federal funds and 81 percent for nonfederal employment programs. Private colleges spent 24 percent of their student employment funds to match federal contributions.[2]

The distinction between federal and nonfederal student employment funds is important because institutions face restrictions in awarding federal funds; even their matching share is thus restricted. Institutions may choose to impose the same restrictions on their own employment programs. Many institutions, in fact, use institutional funds to exceed the 20 percent matching level when federal funds or federal supplements are not sufficient to finance the program through the fiscal year. Some colleges use their own funds to assure year-round employment of students who have been promised jobs under the federal program rather than lay off these students when federal funds fall short. (This predicament is rarely due to changes in federal funding levels. Some institutions simply use their federal allocation faster than planned.) Most institutional student employment funds, however, are awarded with fewer restrictions than are federal funds.

Employment of Students in College Work Programs

Students are employed in all phases of institutional activity. Upperclassmen may assist faculty members by tutoring students or leading discussion sections. Some students provide part-time office

---

2. Data provided by the American Council on Education's Policy Analysis Service and based on the Bureau of Student Financial Aid's analysis of the fiscal operations reports from colleges and universities concerning their campus-based aid programs for the fiscal year 1977.

assistance to departments. Many students are employed in science and computer laboratories or as programming consultants. Libraries employ significant numbers of students in jobs ranging from mundane library surveillance to more sophisticated tasks, including cataloguing and circulation control tasks.

Buildings and grounds crews and campus security forces employ sizable numbers of students, especially in the summer when many renovation, repair, and grounds maintenance tasks must be done. These days it is not unusual to see both men and women students wielding picks and shovels in some campus improvement project. Many students are employed in administrative areas, providing office help, for example, by processing forms in the admissions office; after gaining some experience, these students may develop into skilled admissions counselors. Other students may undertake special studies for various departments or assist with administrative computer programming responsibilities. Athletic departments employ many students as managers and trainers and occasionally even as bus drivers or assistant coaches. Thus, for some students, work experience becomes part of their education.

Students are also hired by various auxiliary enterprises for jobs often associated with work-study programs: washing dishes, busing food trays, serving meals, and counseling in dorms. In addition, many students hold supervisory positions in the cafeteria and bookstore, thus gaining valuable commercial experience. Students may also be employed in related activities, including campus day-care demonstration schools.

The advantage of institutionally funded student work programs is that students with special occupational talents may be employed without the restrictions imposed by federal funds. Many institutions have taken advantage of students who are experienced painters, roofers, and carpenters and who seek part-time or summer employment.

Institutional Benefits of Student Employment

As we have seen, many institutions use institutional funds for student work programs. This use of institutional funds is justified for several reasons.

First, students are less expensive than full-time workers. They are also readily available and can be hired for periods of less than a full year. Until recently, colleges and universities had the option of paying wages slightly below the federal minimum wage to students who were paid from federal funds. Since most institutions try to maintain parity of wages for students paid from both federal and nonfederal funds, starting wages paid to students for many unskilled tasks are below what could be paid to nonstudents. Even when students' wages start at the minimum wage level, institutions have found that prevailing wage rates in surrounding communities (except in certain rural and southern areas) are far enough above the minimum wage rate to make employment of students financially beneficial.

Employment of students, however, is not without financial drawbacks. Supervising students requires special talent and considerable experience. For example, molding a responsible and active campus security force from student workers is rarely an easy task for security directors. Turnover is high. Quality is uneven. Students are hard to find around exam time. Thus, although hiring students may be less expensive for an institution (especially since employee fringe benefits are almost never extended to students), some institutions may have difficulty doing so. Successful student employment projects require campus-wide dedication.

A second reason for offering work-study programs is that the institution can enhance the financial aid package that it can offer students. Most colleges and universities are committed to student employment programs, in spite of the difficulties of supervision mentioned above, and this commitment stems primarily from the desire to assist students in obtaining financial assistance in addition to available grants and loans. Many students who are paid with institutional funds have demonstrated need (the entire amount used to match federal funds goes to students demonstrating need).

Other students may not qualify for many forms of aid, including federal work-study programs. For these students, the burden on the family can often be reduced only, short of a bank loan, by campus work or another job within the community. In addition, students who seek some degree of independence from their parents may make a great effort to minimize their parents' subsidy by working while at college.

A third important reason for hiring students is that many student workers are excellent employees. Many, after two or three years of experience, have developed skills that cannot be easily duplicated by workers hired from the general labor market or by students who qualify for federal employment programs.

Finally, colleges and universities like to hire students because campus employment contributes to a student's education. Students can develop many kinds of skills, including teaching, counseling, managerial, organizational, and interpersonal skills. Many institutions regard the development of these skills in their students as an important part of their mission.

Students' Reasons for Accepting Employment

Students participate in student employment programs for several reasons, some of which have already been mentioned. Now let us examine these reasons from the student's point of view.

Students seek employment during the academic year primarily to earn spending money. Loans and grants are usually devoured by tuition and by room and board. Parents are sometimes reluctant to make up the difference between the bill for the term and any financial aid. Hence, student employment checks are often used for purchasing books, beer, supplies, clothing, food (in addition to that included in a board contract), transportation, and entertainment. Few students earn enough money during the academic year to save for the next term's bill. While in college, some students seek a lifestyle that standard calculations of financial aid do not take into account. Transportation costs, books, and musical instruments can greatly increase student expenses. Many students who do not qualify for federal aid programs are unable to support themselves fully even with contributions from their parents. Thus they are willing to work part time to make up the difference.

Students also work because of the benefits derived from the social interplay that a work setting provides. They enjoy their coworkers, their jobs, and the opportunity to be with people.

Furthermore, students work because of the experience they gain. Employers are interested in the work experience of recent college graduates, and participation in a student employment program may help a student secure postcollege employment.

Finally, students work because they wish to spread their financing of college costs among parental contributions, loans, grants, and work. Students recognize that formulating an aid package entails a trade-off between loans and work. Students therefore accept more work in order to reduce the need for additional loans and, in some cases, the uncertainty of finding available loan funds.

The Need for Institutional Funds

Although the federal government is generous in its allocation of work-study funds, complicated distribution formulas sometimes result in institutions receiving insufficient funds for the work programs they have designed. The institutions may be committed to work programs and may have developed the ability to train students successfully in a wide range of endeavors. Yet they may be unable to secure adequate federal work-study funds.

Many students are disqualified from receiving federal employment funds because of technical violations of federal regulations. For example, prior to the adoption of the Education Amendments of 1980, students attending less than half time were not eligible for federal employment funds. Students who do not make satisfactory educational progress are disqualified. In addition, students who work more than the maximum number of hours allowed in a work week (20 hours during the academic year, 40 hours when classes are not in session) cannot be paid with federal funds for the extra hours. Students who work long work weeks at the beginning of the term so that they may reduce their work commitments as exams approach must be paid with institutional funds.

Discrepancies in the Use of Institutional Funds for Student Employment Programs

According to the statistics given at the beginning of this chapter, public institutions concentrate their institutional aid funds in student employment programs to a greater extent than do private institutions. In addition, the use of institutional funds for these programs varies considerably among institutions of the same type and control. A few private institutions rely to a greater extent on institutional funds for student employment than do most public institutions.

A primary limitation of the use of institutional funds for student employment is the lack of faculty and administrative staff members with the special skills, including patience, needed for the proper direction of student workers. In many cases, a full-time employee is easier to train, remains committed to the job longer, and often is more available during exam periods than are student employees. The constant attention that managers must devote to the development of employee skills requires time and patience. For many students, their participation in the student employment program may be their first work experience, and their level of responsibility and commitment may thus be low. Skilled managers are required to develop and hone a student's work-related skills.

Some institutions have larger institutionally funded work programs than others, moreover, because of the particular character of the student body. At some institutions, fewer students than usual may qualify for federal aid; yet these students may still need more funds than their families can provide. As a result, these institutions are under pressure to provide work for these students.

The socioeconomic status of the student body has much to do with the development of a work ethic on campus. On some campuses, students eschew work. On others, nearly everyone works. This difference in attitudes toward performing relatively menial tasks may partially explain the difference in the use of student employment funds at public and private institutions. Work may be more socially acceptable at public institutions.

Colleges and universities that have recently experienced a period of major growth are also more likely to employ student workers for many tasks. Institutional growth can result in an increase in the availability of new jobs. Occasionally, when the local labor market is unable to provide a sufficient number of full-time employees for these openings, these institutions must develop large student employee programs in order to get the work done. Institutions that have had stable enrollment for several years may be more likely to have already filled many positions with permanent full-time employees. Finally, some institutions—because of tuition, gifts, endowment, or appropriations—are able to provide significant funding for student work programs.

Trends in Institutionally Funded Student Work Programs

We will make two speculations that we hope to confirm in future studies. First, the proportion of institutional student aid funds allocated for work programs will increase at private institutions and will approach the proportion currently allocated by public institutions. As tuition and fees at private institutions increase, students will seek more ways to finance their education. The institutions will assist them by making more work positions available. In some cases, these positions may result from the necessity to cut full-time staff members because of financial difficulties.

Second, we predict that the federal government will make more funds available for work programs and will continue to liberalize eligibility rules to ensure that the extra funds are utilized. The federal work-study program is a popular program that should see growing congressional support.

Tuition and Fee Remissions

Tuition and fee remissions, like student employment programs, benefit both students and institutions. Tuition and fee remissions make up a significant portion of the aid awarded by colleges and universities from their own funds. These remissions often take the form of employee benefits directed toward employees and their dependents. In 1976, institutions gave $101 million in tuition remissions to employees and their dependents; this figure represents 9 percent of all institutionally funded student aid allocated from unrestricted funds.[3] At some institutions, remissions also take the form of cancellation or reduction of tuition for special programs. For example, some schools promote the enrollment of foreign students by offering them in-state tuition. Furthermore, several states have reciprocity arrangements with other states concerning tuition: residents of any cooperating state pay in-state tuition for programs not offered in their home state but offered in another cooperating state. Graduate assistants may also receive tuition remissions as part of their remuneration.

In a recent survey of student aid recipients at independent colleges during the academic year 1979–80, the National Institute of Independent Colleges established three categories of tuition remissions: remissions for employees; remissions for dependents of employees; and all other remissions. According to this survey, the average award to employees receiving a tuition waiver or discount was $1,245, or 24 percent of their total education costs. Tuition and fee remissions or discounts given to dependents of employees averaged $2,290, or 39 percent of their total education costs. All remissions and discounts to persons not related to employees averaged $1,091, or 21 percent of the year's total education costs for those receiving remissions.[4] Tuition reductions, then, are generally substantial.

Tuition remissions, in addition to being an important form of student aid, are often inexpensive employee benefits. The cost to the institution of enrolling an employee's son or daughter is negligible

3. Gomberg and Atelsek, p. 18.

4. Based on Student Aid Recipient Survey Data Base, National Institute of Independent Colleges, Washington, D.C., 1980.

compared to the benefit to the employee of reduced or waived tuition. An extra student in the classroom requires little additional institutional outlay; yet such programs can greatly improve employee loyalty and job satisfaction.

Equity problems may arise because this benefit is available only to employees with family members who qualify. In many institutions, these inequities may be offset by the enormous benefits to low-income employees whose children, without the offer of a tuition waiver, might never have considered attending college. Through tuition remissions, the opportunity for a college education can be extended to persons who may need it most—low-income employees with children of college age.

Tuition remission programs vary. Some institutions restrict eligibility to employees who have worked for a minimum period of time. Other institutions differentiate between faculty and staff members, allowing faculty members to be eligible after a shorter period of employment.

In some cases, institutions have reciprocity agreements with other institutions: cooperating institutions waive tuition for dependents of employees of other cooperating institutions. The expense may be borne either by the employee's institution or by the institution that the employee's dependent attends.

In other cases, institutions pay all, part, or a prescribed amount of tuition charged to the dependents of employees attending *any* institution. These institutions have thus sought to avoid the inequity of allowing only a few employees tuition benefits.

Write-offs

One other form of financial assistance that should be mentioned is the aid given to students who graduate from or leave an institution and who fail to repay all money owed the institution. The amount that American colleges and universities write off yearly as bad debt is unknown. Fiscal officers believe that uncollectible accounts have increased in the last few years, but no surveys have been conducted to estimate the amount written off each year. We estimate that the amount is probably the same as the amount of tuition remissions.

Banks as well as colleges and universities have had difficulty collecting loans, and this difficulty has been well publicized. Institutions are hesitant, however, to reveal how much "aid"— in the form of uncollected current (nonloan) accounts—they give every year because they do not want inadvertently to encourage more delinquency. An increase in unpaid debt indicates that an institution is recruiting students who are less willing to pay for their education. Large uncollectible accounts may also indicate problems in business office collection procedures. In the future, surveys of college and university financial aid programs should give greater attention to this problem.

VI

Institutionally Funded Student Aid and Federal Policy Issues

Through recent legislative initiatives, the federal government has shown increasing interest in institutional policies affecting the amount of institutionally funded student aid awards and the types of students receiving institutional aid. Federal programs relating to higher education reflect the primary areas of the government's interest—the expansion of opportunities for higher education, the promotion of access and choice, and the protection of certain groups of postsecondary education institutions (or "sectors") necessary to maintain access and choice. Institutionally funded student financial aid can complement these federal programs. Likewise, federal programs can encourage or discourage institutions from awarding institutionally funded student aid.

The Pell Grant program demonstrates the federal government's interest in student *access* to higher education. These grants make it easier for a student, regardless of financial background, to obtain a college or university education. The grants are subject to a ceiling defined as the lesser of the following amounts: (1) $1,750 (in fiscal year 1980-81) or (2) half the cost of attending the institution.

Supplemental Educational Opportunity Grants (SEOGs) have promoted student *choice* for higher education. These grants are especially useful to students attending private institutions or high-tuition public institutions. By allowing them a greater choice of institutions, SEOGs assist students who are accepted by more costly institutions and who have financial need.

Other federal programs have significantly aided in promoting access and choice. The guaranteed student loan program, with a subsidy currently estimated at $2 billion, has expanded choice,

65

especially to families with sufficient confidence to borrow. New legislation makes available to parents as well as to students loans at 9 percent interest.

The Developing Institutions program (Title III) shows, to a lesser degree, the federal government's interest in the *survival of the various sectors of higher education*. Legislation has been particularly beneficial to historically black colleges and universities that serve the black community with distinction. Community colleges and small, rural institutions, both private and public, have also benefited from this legislation.

The federal government is also interested in the *efficient use of the resources* it provides to institutions. Cost accounting for research funding is becoming increasingly complex. The federal government is also exerting increasing pressure to tighten financial aid auditing and to improve site visit evaluations for programs such as the Developing Institutions program.

Finally, the federal government has a continuing interest in *improving access, choice, and quality of education in all parts of the country*. Although this concern is not mentioned specifically in any legislative act, most federal appropriations are distributed with this aim in mind. Clearly, Developing Institutions grants and SEOGs are distributed on the basis of state-by-state considerations.

State governments' interests in higher education appear to be somewhat broader. State policies have had a major effect on the awarding of institutionally funded student aid. Differences in tuition between state institutions and independent institutions have compelled some independent institutions to use institutional funds for student aid.

The states are major funders of higher education. Consequently, private institutions and state governments pursue similar objectives. Three areas of mutual concern can be singled out.

1. State governments, like the federal government, are greatly interested in *access*. To promote access, states have created and subsidized extensive public higher education systems, appropriated funds to keep tuition low for public institutions, and implemented state scholarship programs that support many needy students wishing to attend public, private, and, in some cases, even out-of-state institutions.

2. To a much greater extent than the federal government, state governments are interested in the *cost efficiency* of public institu-

tions. Some states make use of complex cost accounting schemes, require occasional line-item budgeting, and even demand personnel position control.

3. State governments are also more interested in the *survival of institutions* than in the survival of sectors. State-supported institutions are clearly within state protection. Several states—New York, Pennsylvania, Illinois, and Maryland, to name a few—have also taken a strong interest in private institutions. Maryland's rescue of the Peabody Institute of Baltimore is a classic example of a state's interest in a specific institution. (The federal government has also indicated an interest in specific institutions, including Meharry Medical College and Eisenhower College. By and large, however, the states have taken more responsibility for individual institutions than has the federal government.)

Institutions share with both levels of government these concerns for access, choice, efficient use of resources, and survival. Nowhere is it stated, however, how these responsibilities are to be shared. In recent decades, as the federal role in higher education has expanded, new student aid legislation has demonstrated the growing willingness of federal policy makers to be responsible for promoting access, choice, and survival. Yet states and institutions are reluctant to relinquish their responsibilities in these areas. Abdicating their prerogatives in any of these areas would result in a loss of control and a loss of their traditional responsibilities.

A key question, therefore, is how the federal government, the state governments, and postsecondary institutions should share these responsibilities. If the federal government takes full responsibility for access and choice, then it may also, in requiring accountability, begin to take responsibility for cost efficiency. The more the federal government becomes the ultimate funder for higher education, the more it will need to dictate the "proper" use of the funds. Institutionally funded student aid, state scholarships, and tuition supplements would be less necessary, but federal control over institutional budgets would increase.

Clearly, the federal government's control of higher education is limited. The federal government has limited revenues, and full financial support of higher education would severely tax the federal budget. Currently, the federal government is being pressured to reduce, not increase, spending for higher education. Even federal programs that boast low net costs and high returns, such as loan supports (which, because of high participation, have high total costs), are under pressure to reduce costs.

In addition, the federal government's ability to administer growing federal financial aid programs is limited. Increased federal support for financial aid to students to guarantee access and choice has led to more concern about student abuses (witness Congress's recent concern about students using financial aid to buy cars) and institutional abuses (most of which reflect poor record keeping rather than actual expenditure abuse). The publicity surrounding these "abuses" reflects a lack of confidence in the bureaucracy to administer even current programs.

The degree of government control of institutional expenditures is related to the proportion of financial support that the government contributes to the institution. Governmental control of expenditures is often insignificant as long as the government believes that an institution has some incentive to control costs on its own. If an institution must raise a portion of its own support, then it has an incentive to control its costs. If an institution raises only a negligible portion of its support, then the incentive to control costs is less compelling.

The federal government's ability to administer a program of full support to guarantee access and choice is severely limited by the individual institution's need to control costs. For this reason, guarantees of access and choice should be shared by institutions, state governments, and the federal government. Institutions must have incentives for controlling costs and ensuring program efficiency. If an institution provides some of its own funds to aid students, then it has an incentive to keep costs low and to make these dollars go further.

State governments face similar limits in their ability to guarantee access and choice. One hindrance is limited revenue sources. Shifts in the economy, reflected particularly in many manufacturing industries, have had a severe impact on the tax revenue of many states. In many states, these revenue losses have been passed on to the higher education system.

Further, full state support of private higher education, it can be argued, would erode the benefits of the current dual education system. Competition between public and private institutions has led to innovation, programs of higher quality, and greater responsiveness by both systems to student needs. Most states lack sufficient revenue to provide full funding for private institutions. In addition, states have an inherent responsibility to protect the competition fostered by the current dual structure.

The Use of Incentives

Although the federal government may wish to improve student access and choice and ensure institutional survival, it lacks sufficient resources to do so. It should then foster cooperation among state and federal agencies and institutions and provide incentives for them to pursue these objectives together. To expand equal opportunity, for example, the federal government should provide some incentives for equitable pricing of higher education.

Equitable pricing dictates that students able to pay for their education should do so, while those unable to do so should be charged lower net costs. The concept of equitable pricing must be tempered, however, with two additional pricing concerns: (1) the benefit of a college education to society versus its benefit to the individual student and (2) the student's present ability to pay versus his or her future ability to pay.

The argument that the federal government should provide incentives to institutions to charge the full cost of an education to those students who are able to pay ignores the fact that much of the benefit of that education accrues to society. An educated populace stimulates productivity, increases tax revenue, and spurs scientific discovery. The social benefit of educating a person argues against charging the full cost of education even to those students who can pay. Some supplements are needed to increase participation in education to the benefit of society as a whole.

On the other hand, a student's present inability to pay full tuititon may not be an indication of his or her ability to pay in the future. While incentives for equitable pricing are of most benefit to low-income families with children in college, many of these students graduate and earn substantially higher wages than their parents. Thus, pricing equity cannot be based solely on a pricing scheme. Pricing equity also requires some price discounting that defers payments to later periods in a student's life when he or she is more sound financially.

Although the issues involved in equitable pricing are complex, the federal government needs to provide incentives to states and institutions to encourage them to maintain equitable pricing schemes. These pricing schemes can be supplemented by federal aid to students and by loans. These supplements must not discourage equitable pricing, however, lest the federal government become fully responsible for access and choice.

Incentives are necessary to oblige institutions to remain cost efficient. Outside agencies cannot assume major responsibility for educational costs unless they have the ability to administer some forms of cost control. Our research indicates that the federal government does not have this capability.

The federal government also needs to provide incentives to institutions to participate fully and fairly in federal and state educational programs. When regulations become too complex or when institutional programs are threatened, cooperation between the federal government and institutions is hurt and the incentive for institutions to assist the federal government in the pursuit of its objectives is reduced.

Federal Policies Affecting Institutionally Funded Student Aid

Institutionally funded student aid has been an important issue in the debate about whether the federal government should provide incentives to institutions to pursue federal interests. The debate has centered around the apportioning of federal student aid, especially SEOGs, distributed by the individual institutions. Federal policy for determining the amount of SEOG funds an instituiton should receive relates to the aggregate unmet financial need of the institution's student body. In computing its aggregate student financial need and, hence, the amount of SEOG funds for which it is eligible, an institution can count 75 percent of costs (including tuition and subsistence) for all aid applicants, minus the total computed contributions from parents and the total BEOG awards. In addition, Congress has stipulated that institutions deduct from aggregate costs their state student incentive grants plus state matching grants and 25 percent of institutional grants.

At issue is the treatment of institutionally funded grants. Should this aid be deducted to determine net aggregate student need? A literal interpretation of the term *net aggregate student need* would require that all institutional grant funds be deducted from total student costs to determine SEOG eligibility. On the other hand, the justification for removing the institutional incentive to provide such aid must be questioned.

The first policy option to be examined is the full penalization of institutions for awarding institutionally funded student financial aid by reducing institutional eligibility for SEOGs at the rate of 100 percent. That is, the SEOG eligibility formula would reduce gross need by each dollar awarded by the institution rather than by 25 percent of each dollar awarded.

Under this policy, clearly, the number and size of institutionally funded student aid awards might decline. Current regulations, however, call for a "maintenance of effort" to prevent institutions from abandoning their aid programs. Institutions could stop further growth of their aid programs and use more work and loans rather than grants to maintain effort, however. They could seek as much federal replacement of institutionally funded awards as possible.

Most likely, fewer federal funds will be available to institutions in the future. Only competition among institutions for these funds would make inflating gross need by reducing institutional aid worthwhile. Institutions awarding large amounts of institutionally funded aid would be at a competitive disadvantage to the extent that they currently depend on SEOGs. Their eligibility would be low, while their aid costs would be high. Moreover, whether the federal government has the fiscal resources even to partially fund the $1.4 billion currently expended in institutionally funded student aid is doubtful.

Given a major disincentive to increase student financial aid from their own funds and less financial support from the federal government, institutions would be under greater pressure to keep tuition down, thus making education inexpensive enough for most students. In turn, institutions will put greater pressure on the federal government to take full financial aid responsibility.

The resolution of this problem could take two forms, depending on the federal government's willingness to assume full responsibility for student access and choice. If the federal government accepts this responsibility, then it will assume a major portion of higher education funding. As a result, its concerns for cost efficiency will increase, and it will probably broaden its demands for cost accountability.

On the other hand, the federal government may refuse to expand programs like SEOG while at the same time providing disincentives for institutions to use their own funds for financial aid. Consequently, the pressures on some private institutions to keep tuition down in the face of rising costs may force a general decline in institutional vitality. The federal government should be concerned about the loss of the incentive to institutions to provide student aid.

The second federal option with respect to SEOG eligibility is to refrain from penalizing institutions at all for awarding student financial aid from their own funds. In this case, the calculation of net student financial need would *not* include a deduction for awards made from the institution's own funds. We predict that institutional reactions to this lack of penalty would be the opposite of those noted above. Institutions would have an incentive to award more institutionally funded student financial aid, and the responsibility for maintaining access and choice would be shared among the federal and state governments and the institutions themselves.

Of course, institutions might also raise tuition to increase eligibility for SEOGs while awarding *all* the extra revenue thus raised in the form of scholarships not deducted from the eligibility formula. Most institutions are not likely to carry the financial game playing to this extreme, however, since high tuition rates, even when offset by special scholarships, tend to discourage many students from applying.

A third option is a compromise that is favored by Congress and that should prove workable. Currently, when institutions determine their SEOG eligibility index, they must deduct from net student costs one-fourth of the aid they award from their own funds.

Institutions that raise tuition and then attempt to offset this tuition increase by awarding institutional scholarships lose a portion of their extra revenue because the amount of SEOGs for which they are eligible is reduced. On the other hand, institutions will have little incentive formerly inspired by SEOGs to reduce institutionally funded student aid, because only a portion of the amount they save by reducing the number of institutional scholarships (25 percent) might be made up by an increase in the amount of SEOG funds for which they are eligible.

Clearly, not all institutions will reason in this fashion. Institutions that have become dissatisfied with their student aid program (perhaps they have found that the program was doing little to increase enrollment) will hold down expenditures on financial aid. These institutions will find that the amount of federal funds for which they are eligible increases by a quarter of the amount of their aid reduction. Thus, the institutions will have more to spend for academic programs (from funds not spent on aid) and will recoup from the federal government a portion of what they spend. Since the amount of student aid funds for which students are eligible is limited, only institutions that award much of their funds on the basis of need will be tempted to reduce their own aid expenditures and hope for some increase in SEOG funds to offset the reduction. Institutions that spend most of their funds on merit-based grants will not necessarily be in a position to replace these funds with federal funds.

Thus, the final option will cause the least amount of change in most institutions' current practices in awarding institutionally funded student aid. Institutions that become dissatisfied with their own student aid programs, however, especially when these programs are largely need-based, may find reason to change their awarding practices.

The Impact of Federal Aid Reductions on Institutionally Funded Student Aid Policies

Each time the federal government reviews student financial aid programs, it comes under pressure to reduce or eliminate all or portions of these programs. Currently, both Congress and the Reagan administration are carefully examining these programs for areas for which funding can be reduced. In order to maintain enrollment levels and to continue to assure equitable access to higher education, many institutions will attempt to replace any lost federal funds with institutional aid awards. Private colleges and universities are likely to feel the impact most directly and to react the most promptly. Selective and nonselective private institutions, however, tend to be affected differently by reductions in federal student aid programs and to react differently.

Selective Institutions

Selective institutions are those institutions that have many more applications for admission than actual openings in the freshman class. Currently, many of these institutions have a policy they describe as "aid-blind" admissions. That is, students are admitted on the basis of their academic and leadership qualifications, not on the basis of financial need. When the institution knows what students will constitute the freshman class, aid is distributed according to need. In many cases, these institutions even meet full need. Whatever need is not met from federal, state, and private sources is made up by the institution from its own funds. Some institutions do not have sufficient funds to make up the full difference and can only meet a portion of full need.

With energy and personnel costs quickly rising and deferred building maintenance programs urgently requiring attention, institutions are finding it ethically difficult to maintain aid-blind admissions. Each year they watch the proportion of their budget alloted for institutionally funded student aid increase. At some point, institutions will find it impossible to raise tuition and rob other projects (such as faculty salaries and building maintenance needs) of funding simply to support the growth of institutionally funded student aid.

Tuition is a limited resource because it cannot grow much faster than family disposable income without affecting the individual's decision about whether he or she can afford to go to college. In fact, tuition growth affects aid growth. Aid must grow both as fast as tuition grows and as fast as the student body broadens economically. As a result, aid expenditures have grown much faster than tuition because of the success of institutions and the federal and state governments in improving access to higher education. Increased tuition is an unlikely source of funds for the student aid needs of institutions.

Federal regulations have contributed to the increase in number of recipients of institutional aid by redefining who is eligible for federal aid, especially with the assistance legislation for middle-income students. Students who at one time were inclined to pay for all their college expenses found that they were eligible for federal aid. They also discovered that the concern for equitable pricing forced institutions to include them under full-need policies. Although the amount of these awards generally has not been large, many students have taken advantage of this legislation.

As long as the total amount of federal and state aid continued to increase, the combined effects of broadened eligibility and improved access for lower-income students could be accommodated without greatly disrupting institutional finances. Now, however, many institutions are near the financial breaking point and have begun to monitor carefully the proportion of their budget that each year must go to institutionally funded student financial aid. Some institutions have set limits to this proportion. If the proportion exceeds the amount specified by current policies, the institution must then consider revising its "aid-blind" admissions policy. Many institutions are approaching this limit.

Decreases in federal aid programs will push these institutions over the edge, forcing them to choose between equality of access and quality of programs. A drop in the maximum BEOG award (or even increases that fail to keep up with inflating institutional costs) will require larger allocations of institutional aid funds or major decreases in the proportion of need met by the institution for all students. The federal government can decrease the amount of student loan funds by making loans more costly for banks to handle or by making them an economically infeasible gamble for low-income students. If the government chooses to do so, institutions will find that, without institutional supplements, the average student aid package will fall far short of meeting full need.

Selective institutions must then choose one of the following alternatives: (1) they can maintain aid-blind admissions and their current policies of meeting full need (or a large percentage of need) by raising tuition or cutting other programs; (2) they can continue aid-blind admissions but drastically reduce the amount of aid they award even to the most needy students; or (3) they can end aid-blind admissions and admit only those students they can afford to fund with institutional aid.

Selective institutions are not likely to choose the first alternative. They may not be able to raise tuition or further cut programs. To do so would harm the majority of their students, for the quality of education would slip while its cost would increase beyond what is now considered reasonable for those who can afford to pay.

Nor would these institutions likely choose to tolerate the trauma caused by the second alternative—admitting students who had little chance of finding the funds to pay. Students would be caught part way through their education owing the institution large sums and facing dismissal for unpaid bills. The institution itself would be stuck with the unpaid bills.

The most likely recourse for most institutions is the third alternative—to limit the number of students with severe financial need admitted to the institution. The ethical dilemma is having to decide whether to discriminate against some poor students by not admitting them or whether to admit them now and later have to deny them the right to continue their education. Institutions could still admit students with need, but only within restricted quotas.

Less Selective Private Institutions

These institutions accept the vast majority (in most cases, more than 90 percent) of all applicants. If the federal government does decrease its funding of student financial aid, then the survival of these institutions may be threatened.

The choices that less selective private institutions have are even more limited than those that selective institutions have. Admissions policies are more than aid-blind: admissions are open. Tuition is lower at these institutions to allow a broader range of clientele and to allow federal, state, and private programs to pay for as much of the student financial need as possible. If aid from these sources declines, then the institution's net price will, in effect, increase.

Increasing tuition to allow extra student aid funds to be awarded to needy students is not an option for these institutions. First, enrollment is likely to fall as costs increase. Second, at many of these institutions, the great majority of the students *are* on financial aid—there simply are no "rich" students to tax. In many cases, the few students most affected by an increase in net price would be the very ones that the institution finds most desirable.

These institutions must attempt either to continue to attract students (even though these students must pay greatly increased costs) or to cut costs and programs further and reduce the net price. In either case, enrollment is likely to fall. Declines in enrollment mean that revenue will also decline and that further cuts will be necessary. The spiral started by the shift in federal student aid funding is likely to alter drastically institutional financial viability. According to data from the National Center for Education Statistics collected from its HEGIS financial surveys, 35 percent of all private institutions have liabilities that outweigh assets to the extent that they cannot be covered by their endowment. These institutions show evidence of continuing deficits and will be least able to weather cuts in federal student aid. Thus, a large proportion of private postsecondary institutions could face great financial uncertainty.

Federal aid to colleges and universities can be both too much and too little. The most effective policies call for encouraging institutionally funded student aid programs because of their great value in meeting national higher education objectives. Federal, state, and institutional policy makers must maintain their partnership in pursuing the objectives of access, choice, and institutional survival through the use of student financial aid. If the federal government, state governments, or the institutions themselves decline to participate in student aid programs, these goals are threatened.

Appendix
Federal Student Aid Programs

The following definitions are based on the program descriptions found in *Annual Evaluation Report on Programs Administered by the U.S. Office of Education, Fiscal Year 1979* (Washington, D.C.: Office of Education and Office of Evaluation and Dissemination, U.S. Department of Health, Education, and Welfare, 1980).

BEOG—Now called Pell Grants, formerly Basic Educational Opportunity Grants. Awarded to students on the basis of need up to the maximum amount of need or half the cost of education, whichever amount is lower. Decision to award is based on a need formula and is unrelated to any other federal grant to the institution.

CWS—College Work Study. A program under which the federal government pays 80 percent of the wages of eligible student workers; the institution pays the other 20 percent. Eligibility is determined by need. Less-than-half-time students are not eligible. Grants are made by the federal government to the institution for distribution.

GSL—Guaranteed Student Loans. Loans to students attending eligible institutions of higher education. This program is designed to utilize nonfederal loan capital supplied primarily by commercial lenders but also by some educational institutions and state and private agencies acting as direct lenders. These loans are guaranteed either by individual state or private nonprofit agencies (reinsured by the federal government) or directly by the Department of Education.

NDSL—National Direct Student Loan. The federal government funds 90 percent of these loans; the institution funds the remaining 10 percent through matching grants. These loans are for students with need. No interest is charged while the student is seeking a degree, and the interest is generally low thereafter (3–4 percent). Twenty-year repayment, hardship deferrals, and payment cancellations for certain kinds of public service are available.

SEOG—Supplemental Educational Opportunity Grants. SEOGs are grants to assist in making available the benefits of postsecondary education to qualified students who, for the lack of financial means, would be unable to obtain such benefits without such a grant. The funds are provided by the federal government, while the awards are made by the institution.

SSIG—State Student Incentive Grant Program. The SSIG program is designed to encourage states to develop or expand programs of grant aid to help undergraduate students with "substantial financial need" who attend eligible postsecondary institutions. SSIGP is a program funded equally by the federal and state government. Under this program federal funds are allotted to the states on the basis of a formula reflecting current student attendance patterns. Disbursements are made directly by the federal government to the states and then by the states to postsecondary institutions on behalf of students. While states are responsible for the selection of grant recipients, selection criteria are subject to review by the Commissioner. Individual student grants are limited to $2,000 per academic year.